# *The Releasing Strategy*

## *for Personal Power and Peace of Mind*

Blessings to you Skip – Sharon Cameron

By

**SHARON MARSHALL CAMERON**

First Edition

**WATERSHED BOOKS**

San Jose, California

# The Releasing Strategy
# for Personal Power & Peace Of Mind.

**By Sharon Marshall Cameron**

Published by:

Watershed Books
2059 Camden Ave. #249
San Jose, Ca 95124     (408) 978-3006


First Printing, March, 1993
Printed in the United States of America

Cover design: Catherine Pierce Moyers

Library of Congress Catalog Number 93- 93813
Cameron, Sharon Marshall
The Releasing Strategy For Personal Power and Peace Of Mind
by Sharon Marshall Cameron
Includes index.

ISBN 0-9635820-6-2 $11.95 Softcover, Canada $14.95

## *Dedication*

*This book is dedicated to you, the reader, and to your hopes and aspirations. I sincerely hope you will find the technique I present here the wonderfully useful tool it can be.*


## Acknowledgments

I give blessings and thanks to my husband, Clark Cameron, who has lived the development of this book and the technique with me. This book is an outgrowth of our experience and knowledge.

Thanks also go to Dr. David Cheek and Leslie LeCron for their immense contribution to the knowledge of the inner mind, and for the development of the hypnotherapeutic technique that has become part of the foundation of ***The Cameron Method.***

Thanks to Harry McClusky, and Peg Stewart for publication assistance, and to Catherine Pierce Moyers for cover graphics.

And, especially, I give thanks to all our clients and students through the years. It has been through working with you that we have learned so much. Your successes have provided the stairway for others to climb.

## *The Releasing Strategy*

### Contents

**Introduction**

# Why Should You Read This Book?

Should you bother with one more book about your inner mind, and how you might change it? Could this one really differ from any others? You may feel you have already tried just about everything to make the changes you want. The methods offered might work for someone else, but maybe not for you.

Perhaps you can't visualize, or meditate for the hours it takes for real improvement, let alone attain *enlightenment*, whatever that may mean. You may have been able to get key ideas intellectually, but haven't been able to put those concepts to work at the inner emotional level to have life-long impact.

In Western Society, we have often wanted to realize instant benefits from Eastern philosophy and methods. Our *fast-food thinking* leads us to believe we should be able to reach enlightenment, or at least temporary Nirvana, in a weekend workshop.

Certainly, by the time we have read through an entire book or taken a course, we should have it! We should be happy, able to create what we want, and keep our balance in any circumstance. And, of course, we should be able to create love, health, and wealth in our lives.

Wanting this enlightenment, we have parroted the est

phrase, *I got it!* Most participants, however, having used the words to invoke the reality, go home after the experience without *it.* The enthusiasm of the group effort can wane in a short time.

Is it so wrong to keep searching for this golden fleece? We even look for it in the movies and TV as we cheer on the hero (our real selves) to overcome impossible odds.

I don't think we are wrong to keep looking. With the characteristic naiveté of our culture, Americans have often come up with solutions to problems long thought insoluble. We know that just because something hasn't been done before doesn't mean we can't do it now.

This fact accounts for the development of this method and the writing of this book. *The Releasing Strategy* is a method by which you can actually accomplish, or at least free yourself to accomplish, what you really want in life, almost instantly.

Thus, we meet the most essential requirement before we even begin! If you can read, or if someone else can read this to you, and if you *follow the simple directions*, you can learn right now how to let go of unconscious blocks that may be limiting or frustrating you in any area of life.

No longer will you have to go to a *shrink,* or spend years on a couch, or in meditation, or studying all the learned thinkers of the world. Now, I didn't say you shouldn't do those things, just that you don't *have to* in order to accomplish what you want.

Great truths are often simple, and the foundation of this method rests squarely on simple truths. The method itself is simple, fast, and usually interesting. It may not always be easy, but then, you do still want some challenge in life, don't you?

We have named this method of empowerment, The Releasing Strategy. We have found it incorporates both masculine and feminine elements of the psyche. The usual methods for reaching and changing the inner mind are right-brain: feminine and intuitive. They leave the left-brain Western mind adrift as it wants to *do* something, which gets it nowhere. In our formula, *Releasing* represents the feminine, and *Strategy* the masculine mode of goal-seeking action.

As I will demonstrate in later chapters, using *The Releasing Strategy* engages the whole brain, or the whole person. Although Releasing is a feminine approach to problem solving, the activation element is the masculine, or assertive part of the personality that engages the will. In being *willing* to release a negative belief, perception or judgment, we decide through our conscious ego that it is best for us to change our minds about an issue.

Here lies the one part of *The Releasing Strategy* that may prove difficult or, sometimes insurmountable. You may have so much of your identity invested in your current beliefs, regardless of facts or consequences, that you are unwilling to change. You may feel *willing to die first.*

The basis of this unwillingness to change is fear. When you are angry, resentful or fearful, there is a part of you that wants to hang onto these feelings in the belief that they will somehow protect you. You may have the common conviction that fear is both armor and weapon. I know it doesn't feel like fear when you want to punch someone in the nose in order to teach them or change them to your way of thinking, but it is.

You can believe it is justifiable to wage unlimited war if you are defending yourself against what you consider attack. Why else would we call our federal government's former War Department, the Department of Defense? This, of course, is the section of the government whose primary job is to scan the world in search of reasons to be fearful, and wage war against them.

Your mind harbors no small supply of fear and its alter ego, anger. Have you ever noticed how, in a heated argument, as your voice is raised, your breathing is faster, and your body shifts into an attack stance? You could call it a defense stance. They look the same.

When someone gets hurt in such a clash, often through no premeditated thought by either party, it just seems at the moment there is no other way to react.

The lesson, you may have noticed, is that your fear threatens those you fear, for the same reasons your opponents' fear threatens you. The basic response to fear is fight or flight, and you can never be certain which response those who fear you will choose.

Wouldn't it be a blessing to have a simple, workable method of changing your reactions so you would not be hurt or hindered by your own unconscious triggered responses? You can gain this benefit from this book. You can learn not only to change your reactions, you can actually learn to remove the major cause of negative reactions to you and what you do.

You can finally have something new and different, a verbal process that is simple, fast and able to lift the unconscious limits in your inner mind.

This same process enables you to release the fears and hostile feelings that cause negative reactions in other people and contribute to other undesirable outcomes. In this way, *The Releasing Strategy* offers lasting positive impact on your self image and on both personal and professional relationships.

So, try it! Take a chance, and join me in the fascinating new experience that is yours when you learn to let it go with *The Releasing Strategy.*

## Chapter 1

# Birth of a Strategy for Change

*The Releasing Strategy* is part of a system for mental change that my husband, Clark Cameron, and I have developed and have been working with for the past 13 years.

We have called our process *Response Therapy:The Cameron Method* because we use it to change responses that are creating negative attitudes running people's lives. We also acknowledge our use of ideomotor or biofeedback responses to identify the inner mind causes of those attitudes.

In *Response Therapy:The Cameron Method*, we retrieve the actual reasons causing blocks or limits directly from your inner mind and then lead you through the Release of those negative assumptions or beliefs. In other words, as in a friendly computer program, you can delete the negative and keep the good. You get an intensely personal look at, and are able to get control of, the often hidden forces that have been running your life.

*The Releasing Strategy* is the way we change negative inner assumptions in Response Therapy. We have presently trained only a handful of people to be facilitators using the total process. Since we can only work with a relatively small portion of the people who could benefit from it, I have been moved, or rather driven, to write this book for anyone who will take the time to read about it and apply *The Releasing Strategy* as I teach it here.

I will not go in depth into the full process of *Response Therapy:The Cameron Method,* as it is much more involved than it sounds. My husband, Clark, is writing a manual on the total process including accessing the inner mind, doing the analysis to pinpoint the causes of problems, then using *The Releasing Strategy* to let go of those reasons. It is titled, *Becoming Your Authentic Self.* My goal here is to share with you *The Releasing Strategy* for creating inner change, so you can have this powerful, useful tool to control and improve your own day-to-day responses.

We have found you don't always have to know exactly what caused the negative thought or attitude in order to get rid of it. The reasons, or at least the more obvious justifications, will pop into your head when you ask "Why?" in your own mind. For example, you might ask, "Why am I so angry with my mother?" What will come up is the justification for that anger. "She just nagged at me again." Note the *again* and you will get a clue that the real basis is your belief that *she always nags me.* Perhaps she hurt your feelings when she nagged you over being late, being messy, being inconsiderate, or not loving her enough.

We are also developing computer software that will be able to lead you through the questioning process. The presence of a therapist or facilitator (or computer) who is not caught up in your feelings and emotions can be crucial to the success of the analysis portion of the process.

If you follow the instructions in this book, however, you will gain a lifelong technique for controlling the contents of your inner mind. With it, you can do a better job of controlling the outer life you are producing.

To help you understand *The Releasing Strategy* and *The Cameron Method*, I must include a little background on my relationship with my husband and how we happened to develop the method. It is an unusual story in itself.

In 1978, I was newly divorced, a resident of Atlanta, Georgia with my three children, then aged 16, 13, and 9. We lived in a large suburban home with a half-acre, woods and stream behind. This was and still is typical of many homes in Atlanta.

I was enjoying my new independence, and was working at the Unity Church there. I had been very much involved in psycho-spiritual studies for many years. These studies had now led to my teaching a class at the church on *Creating Your Own Reality.*

In December, 1978, a man named Clark Cameron came to Atlanta from San Francisco on a promotional tour. He "happened" to call Unity, and I "happened" to answer the phone. He asked what was going on at the church that night, and found that only my class was meeting. He came to the class, we met, we got together and later married. Our lives and the lives of quite a few other people have been changed because of it.

Clark is an interesting and brilliant person. He is a scientist, scholar, inventor and a thinker who has often been many years ahead of his time. At times that last characteristic has not made for the most comfortable life, nor always being easily understood. When we met he had developed the psychological system using the inner mind accessing technology of what has become *Response Therapy: The Cameron Method.*

This uses what we call the Response Monitor, or simply Monitor, for short. It is a weight on a line, or a pendulum. Using it we can get coded responses from the inner mind of a client while he or she holds it by the fingertips. It is a feedback device we use to monitor the inner mind, hence the name. Clark learned this accessing method from David Cheek, M.D., Gyn., a renowned clinical hypnotherapist, then practicing in San Francisco, since retired.

The Monitor works as a form of ideomotor response, meaning a motor response based on an impulse from the inner mind. With his partner, clinical psychologist Leslie LeCron, now deceased, Cheek had written a landmark book on hypnotherapy called *Clinical Hypnotherapy* (Grune & Stratton, N.Y., 1968). In their book, they extensively document the use of ideomotor responses.

More recently, clinical psychologist Ernest Rossi has collaborated with David in writing an in depth overview of the latter's 40 years of clinical hypnotherapy, and use of ideomotor responses. This newer book is called *Mind-Body Therapy* (W. W. Norton, N.Y., 1988).

Clark added an immensely important new dimension to the use of the Monitor. He used the Monitor to measure the percentage of inner mind positive as well as negative feelings about specific individuals, ideas or experiences. This procedure can also be used to measure the percentage of fear you have of anything or anyone.

In Atlanta, we developed a workshop we called *Breakthrough.* In it we used the Monitor to determine the status of negative emotions or blocks then used a visualization process of forgiveness to clear the inner mind of them.

We might have kept on doing those workshops indefinitely if we hadn't decided to attend an *est* seminar. Clark had worked with many est graduates in San Francisco and had been very successful helping them get "unstuck" from continuing problems. *est* (Erhard Seminar Training now called The Forum) was then the most successful consciousness seminar in the country. We felt they must be doing something right. We decided to attend because we felt we could learn how to communicate better about our own workshop .

At *est* we both had to let go of our initial negative reactions to their processes. We felt that their conscious mind rhetoric was unnecessary, since we had a better way of changing the inner mind. Once we accepted the fact that we were attending their seminar and not ours, however, we mostly enjoyed the two weekends.

It was at the "graduation" session that we were appalled to realize that the same leaders who had been in effect hypnotizing the group for two weekends were directly using that influence to sell graduate seminars. We looked at each other in agreement as Clark said, "Let's get out of the seminar business."

We had both realized that high pressure selling was necessary to sell seminars to the public, and neither of us wanted to do it. We believed in our workshop, but we believed more that it was unethical to manipulate another person's consciousness. So there we were, with an effective group process, and not willing to do what we felt was needed to sell it.

Clark later used his visualization process in an audiocassette album he created called *Permanent Weight Loss.* It was published in 1982 by the Nightingale-Conant Corporation, the world's largest publisher of audiocassette albums. It was their first publication of any visualization process, and they referred to it as "audio-imaging." While producing the album for Nightingale Conant, we developed *The Releasing Strategy*, to which Clark refers in one of the tapes.

The basis of *The Releasing Strategy* was brought to us in a strange way. One day a young man called and asked if he could come see us. I don't know how he had heard of us, but he was the inspired agent who would put us in touch with the then missing element of *Response Therapy:The Cameron Method*, and what has become the theme of this book.

After our initial get-acquainted conversation, he confessed he didn't really know why he was there. He said he felt *guided* to come see us. We were polite, and as we continued to chat with him he mentioned a "Doc" Lindwall, and his work. When he learned we had never heard of Doc Lindwall, he smiled and said, "Oh, that must be why I'm here."

Lindwall was a chiropractor and Concept Therapist in Atlanta. He was working with muscle testing and intuition to help ascertain patient's needs. He had been moved to have patients say releasing phrases and had found it had helped them greatly. Our visiting friend couldn't tell us anything so simple however, and if he had we probably wouldn't have made the connections we later did. He simply said, "You have to meet this man."

We ended up spending the Fourth of July weekend alone with "Doc" and his wife Ruth at their retreat in the Georgia mountains. He demonstrated his use of releasing phrases on both of us. We were impressed and immediately wondered if it could work to change the precise emotional programming obtained with our accessing method.

The visualization process Clark had developed was exceptionally good, but it depended on the client's ability to visualize, and took time. Releasing, on the other hand, works immediately.

My contribution at this point was that we should use the words, *belief, perception, and judgment* in *The Releasing Strategy* because that's how the programming initially gets in there. You have a belief, based on a perception, and then you make a judgment that becomes part of your inner mindset. With this new approach, we now had the final element of what has become *The Releasing Strategy*.

No longer needing a workshop format or visualization to help people handle their underlying problems, I started working with individuals. Using the Monitor to access their inner beliefs and blocks, I then used *The Releasing Strategy* to change them. I worked out of our home at first, then out of two separate offices of doctor friends who were supportive of the work.

At this point, we had a wonderful, effective therapy and no name for it. One of my clients told me of an excellent counselor and professional astrologer, named David Railey, in Atlanta. I had read of him in previous years when he was featured in newspaper articles. He had gained an outstanding reputation and had many clients using his services to assist them with business and the stock market.

I felt that if David were to be aware of what I did, he would be a source of referrals. I made an appointment to share our new process with him. I still have the tape of that meeting.

There was a strange electricity in the air as we met and talked about the process, and he told me he was good with names and felt he could come up with the right name for it. Shortly, he smiled and asked, "Why not call it *Response Therapy: The Cameron Method?*" And we did!

When David made his suggestion, there was no sound in the room other than our voices, but when played back, there was a crackling-like static on the recording of it. It sounds like the electricity we felt in the air around us. It was a very exciting moment.

After a few years of work in Atlanta, Clark went to Los Angeles to help his mother and aunt (both in their late eighties) to move into a nursing home. He had always talked of eventually moving back to California. While he was there again, a meeting with the president of a company led him to work individually with its salesmen to increase their success. They were so happy with the results that the management referred sister companies and I flew out to work with him.

He decided in short order that it was time to relocate in California. He had also been talking about translating our process into an interactive computer program. I had always rejected this idea as I felt that so much of what was accomplished was through the intuition of the therapist or facilitator.

However, now we both felt led to be in California, closer to Silicon Valley where we could find the people with the expertise to accomplish computerizing the process. Many people could benefit rather than just the handfuls we could reach individually.

We established a practice in San Jose in the Silicon Valley in 1985. Since then, we have had a therapy practice that has hardly ever been too busy because we have regularly gone through clients so fast. They have come mostly from word of mouth referrals, and working in two or three hour sessions, finished the process usually within 5 to 10 meetings. When I say finish the process, I mean we get their inner minds clear of the negative beliefs and blocks about everyone and everything important to them. No, they do not lose their memory. They simply lose the negative energies and limits that have been holding them back in any life area.

This has been accomplished for many people who had previously been in all kinds of therapy or self-development efforts, as well as for people who have had no previous work.

If you would like to prove for yourself that *The Releasing Strategy* works to change your own feelings and reactions when you use it, please refer to Chapter 16 on fears. In that chapter, on page 121, I give a demonstration that you can use with yourself and a friend. You can physically prove the reaction.

Until the computer programs are generally available, I want to share with you what you can accomplish on your own, without a facilitator of any kind. Since we have dealt with so many different kinds of problems over the years, I can lead you in this bookwith *The Releasing Strategy* to overcome many of your own life challenges.

In the following chapters, I will teach you how to let go of the negatives that may be holding you back in important areas of your life. Come along with me and discover that the most exciting adventures of life can begin when you gain control of your own mind and emotional reactions, and find the freedom that results.

## Chapter 2

# The Mind Lever

*The Releasing Strategy* is a tool you can use to lift out or let go of blocks and limits in your mind. It is deceptively simple, but then so is a lever. So, you might say, Releasing is a lever to lift off the weights that are dragging you down, or holding you back in any area of life.

Releasing is simply saying, preferably out loud, a statement of acceptance that a particular belief or judgment is no longer true for you. I say "no longer", because the statement is tied to a negative belief you have had that is causing you problems. We believe it is the first really new and effective consciousness-changing process in many years. It is neither an affirmation nor a visualization process.

In some systems of thought, Releasing might be classified as a denial of a negative. As we use it, it is much more than a simple denial. It has become part of a whole new system for changing the inner mind.

Having this fabulous technique has been somewhat of a frustrating experience. I have found over and over, as I have worked with individuals, that *The Releasing Strategy* works. It is a powerful verbal method to free your mind from the negative influences that seem to bombard both from without and within. I unreasonably expect everyone to understand that it works and to use it.

However, in this world, I have found that even though you may understand consciously that something is useful, or works for other people, you can resist or not see its usefulness for you. If you do that, of course, you won't use it.

For me it has too often been like having diamonds and gold in my hands and not being able to show them to anyone, or finding that they are invisible after all.

I also believe that we have discovered something powerful that will have as high an impact on consciousness techniques as the discovery of affirmations. *The Releasing Strategy* is one of the world's best-kept-secret weapons you can have in playing the game of life.

Affirmations, or positive statements of belief, have been used a long time and many books have been written about using them. They were first publicized widely in this country by the French pharmacist Emil Coué in the 1920's, creating a popular fad of the day and becoming one of the underpinnings of most "positive thinking" philosophies.

As Coué promoted it, people could create a better life by repeating. "Every day, in every way I am getting better and better"— or, "My life is getting better and better," etc.

The use of a statement of belief, or affirmation, is an attempt to implant that belief in the inner mind. In hypnosis this type of learning is called an imprint. We will discuss imprints in more detail later.

An affirmation usually must be repeated over and over and can work if there isn't too much resistance to it in the inner mind. However, if there is that resistance, it is like rain falling on your mental roof. It simply bounces off as if it hadn't even been said; it is as if the subconscious replies "baloney" (or worse) to each affirmation.

In our experience, there are at least two reasons why affirmations do not always work as well as they should. First, they always go against your real beliefs. You affirm something to be true about yourself or your life that is currently not so. (Otherwise, why would you be affirming it?)

You do not see athletes repeating, "I am healthy!" unless they happen to be injured or sick; nor do you find even the greatest devotees of Positive Self-Talk repeating each morning, "The sun is rising! The sun is rising!" in an effort to raise the sun. (Of course, we might do that if we believed the sun wasn't going to rise!)

The second reason affirmations may not work is that we all seem to believe negative thoughts more eagerly than we do positive ones. Possibly from a lifetime of disappointment, we expect to fail, to lose, to have pain, to lose love, satisfaction, justice or good.

That is called being "realistic." It is certainly understandable that when you experience more loss than gain in life, you may accept the belief that "that's the way it is — and ever more shall be."

The very reasons you can have so much trouble with affirmations, however, are the same reasons why *The Releasing Strategy* works! It is like the *reverse* of an affirmation. If you can say it, simply SAY IT, and it hits the belief squarely, you can remove a problem or judgment with one statement.

The technique works as though you are holding your belief tightly in your hand, then put your arm out and let it go! It's rather like dropping it through a trap door.

You may have to say it in different ways, since the inner self may have the idea implanted in different ways, but you won't have to repeat the very same statement as you would an affirmation. With *The Releasing Strategy*, you can actually remove the stumbling blocks and limits from your inner mind.

We often have people ask why you don't have to affirm the positive after you have released the negative beliefs. It seems that if you have negative opinions about anything in your inner mind, you also have an underlying base of positive about it. To put it in spiritual terms, our true nature is love, not fear.

In working with clients, we have found that there are basically two emotions: love and fear. Love is what underlies all the positive emotions – joy, goodness, loyalty, friendship, beauty, light and progress in humanity.

Fear is the emotion behind pain, sorrow, hate anger, attack, darkness and devolving of the soul. It generates two basic responses: fight or flight. Fight is the attack side of fear. No sane person will attack anything or anyone unless they believe they are defending themselves or someone or something they believe in. You must believe in the attack, also.

The other outcome is the flight response. This is obviously fear. Attack is seldom recognized as a fear response, but it is as fearful as a cornered animal is fearful.

Even when you consider an attack on a small country by a more powerful one, like the Iraqi attack on Kuwait, if you look more closely you will find the fear. Saddam Hussein was very much in debt from his war on Iran, and was afraid he would lose power if he had to take responsibility for the economy of his country, and the loans he had to repay to Kuwait as well as others. It seemed a sensible response to him, I'm sure, to the threat of his loss.

The world runs on varying degrees of these fear responses: anger, guilt, sorrow, pain, resentment, and criticism. Wherever someone or something should be different, in our belief, we attack them or ourselves over that variance in our perception.

Speaking of "*should*," I'd like to point out that only unhappiness comes from your "shoulds" or "shouldn't haves." If you believe something or someone in your life *should have been* different, or behaved differently, you can rail against your experience, impotently, or seek revenge, which, alas, will not restore any previous status quo.

We experience our true helplessness as we do this. The hard fact is, if we, or they, or it *could* have been different, then we or they, or it *would* have been.

However, if it was as it was, then it *could not* have been different! My husband Clark loves to say "History does not disclose its alternatives." So how do we get ourselves so upset about it all? Easily, mightily, and eternally. We, as the human race, carry on this way and progress in spite of ourselves.

The cause of this progress may be that we do have the ability, and occasionally the willingness, to learn from our mistakes. But we learn from our mistakes, not our regrets or should-have-beens.

Edison is quoted as saying when asked how he could keep working when he had failed thousands of times to invent the electric light, "I have found thousands of ways not to do it." If he had thought he "should have" invented it by then, he would certainly have stymied himself long before he accomplished his goal.

To change inner mind negatives in *Response Therapy*, we use several types of Releasing introductions or prefaces. Our general favorite, and the most powerful, is:

**I release my belief, perception and judgment that ...**

We use this as the operational phrase prefacing a negative belief that we have obtained from a client's inner mind. For example, I may ask you to repeat after me, "**I release my belief, perception and judgment** that my father loved my brother more than me."

We have worded the statement to correspond to the way you, the client, inserted the unhelpful program in the first place. You had a belief, based on your perception at some point in time, and then you judged the perception to be negative, or harmful in some way, and especially – *true*.

The Bible is very clear in Jesus' instruction to "judge not, lest you be judged." As a species though, we seem to be addicted to it. We busily judge events, situations, and people as either good or bad, and immediately put them accordingly into our subconscious data banks. The negative beliefs seldom end up helping us, and often do hurt us as we project them out into our current and future relationships and actions.

Other Releasing Statements from *Response Therapy* are these:

**I release all need or desire to ...**

(This gets to the motivational basis of an inner mind program.)

... feel he hates me.

... feel upset about my father.

... keep hating my brother.

And there is the other motivational release:

**I release all unwillingness to ...**
... forgive my father.
... change my habits.

Finally, the release for the bottom line of all negatives is directed squarely at fear:

**I release all fear ...**

... that my father didn't love me as much as he loved my brother.
...that I am unlovable.

These statements are deceptively simple. As you run into a negative belief and try to say the statement, I suggest you will find that they are not as easy to say as they seem.

We constantly have clients choke up, prove unable to hear the statement they are supposed to repeat, and/or say the statement with a 180 degree twist to change it without consciously realizing it. They may say, for instance, "**I release my belief, perception and judgment** that my father *didn't* love my brother more than me."

In this book, you can learn to use *The Releasing Strategy* with your own negative thoughts, and free yourself for a happier existence with other people, with yourself, and with your life.

So, let's get started this moment. First, repeat aloud...

**I release my belief, perception and judgment …**

… that changing my inner beliefs can't be so simple!

**I release all unwillingness …**

… to become a stronger, better, healthier, happier person using *The Releasing Strategy.*

**I release all fear …**

… of letting go of negative inner beliefs.

**I release all fear …**

… of changing.

Say these statements aloud correctly and you're on your way! If you find you don't want to repeat these statements aloud, you have a wonderful opportunity to learn something important about yourself.

Ask yourself: How do I benefit from believing I can't change my inner mind so easily? How does it help me to be unwilling to become a happier person? Then, after you have the reasons that float up to justify your position – pry them out with your mind lever by Releasing those too!

## Chapter 3

# Keys to Your Inner Mindset

*The Releasing Strategy* works with the natural way that negative or other beliefs and perceptions get into your mind in the first place. These pathways to emotional programming were first documented by Dr. David Cheek and Leslie LeCron in their book, *Clinical Hypnotherapy*, mentioned earlier. They classified them as seven keys. We have expanded them to nine.

When we last saw Dr. Cheek, he said that he felt all the keys could ultimately be reduced to just one, the Imprint, and we agree with him. Since I want to teach you to notice the different ways you may be unknowingly influencing yourself, however, it is more useful to detail them first. Quite simply, they are ways in which you are emotionally affected by your interaction with your environment and by your own thoughts.

Our first such learning is done through the process called **Identification**. We identify with role models, parents, or other "big people" when we are little. With this unconscious mechanism we learn our language, mannerisms, prejudices, and so much more.

There was a best-seller self-awareness book published in 1977, titled *My Mother Myself: The Daughter's Search For Identity,* by Nancy Friday. It leads the reader to the sometimes upsetting realization that as adults we are so often unconsciously replaying our mother or father. Your first instruction on how to view the world was was from the standpoint of your parents' attitudes about it, especially the attitudes of the parent of your own sex.

**Disidentification** is the other side of the coin. You may disidentify with an alcoholic parent, or child beater, or critic, or loser, saying "I'll never be like that." But, as you have focused on the negative, you may be drawn into reproducing the behavior. "He who would struggle with a serpent," wrote Frederick Nietzsche, "must beware lest he become one."

One of my clients came to me after alienating his family. His ex-wife and his grown children would have nothing to do with him. He had two daughters and one son. He had beaten the son regularly throughout the boy's childhood, and the only reason he finally stopped it, was because his wife divorced him. Now the son was in his twenties and the father was trying to make amends to him by employing him in his business. Their relationship was still immensely strained.

The man was ridden with guilt. He loved his son and thought he had been raising him appropriately. Now, he was close to bankruptcy in his business, couldn't concentrate and was depressed.

I worked with him to find why he had needed to beat the son, especially when he never beat the daughters. When his inner mind revealed the main reason was Identification, we reviewed his own childhood.

He had grown up in rural Georgia with a father who beat him regularly. He told me that when he went to school, he had pulled his short pants down to cover up the welts that were on his legs from the whippings he had received. I asked him if it ever occurred to him that the other children may not have been treated that way. Of course he said, "never." This man had gone through childhood experiences he hated, and yet typically, when he grew up into the father role himself, he performed as he had been trained.

This is how much very dysfunctional human behavior is naturally passed along from generation to generation. It always seems to the affected individuals that *they are doing the right thing*.

The second key to emotional programming is the **Imprint** mentioned in the previous chapter. An imprint is an instant learning experience, through words you tell yourself or hear from a significant or important other person. Imprints, however, are not limited to words. They can result from something you saw, or felt, or heard, or thought. Books, movies and TV can also be a source of imprints.

The movie *Psycho* imprinted many people through the gruesome murder of Janet Leigh's character in a motel shower. More than one of my male clients has told me that he would not take a shower in a motel without locking the door of the bathroom. This was twenty-some years after seeing the movie! I was also amazed since I hadn't thought that it would have affected men so strongly. Hitchcock was a genius! Because he was as good as he was, we have an imprinted generation.

Another movie, *Jaws,* had such a strong imprinting effect that it kept many people away from the seashore for a long time. Even when people went back to swim, many did not feel comfortable going out past wading depth. And all many of us have to hear is a few beats of the accompanying music to set our hair on end! Remember, the next time you are totally engrossed in a book or movie, watch out for imprints!

People in advertising have long understood the importance of imprints. They seek to imprint us with such slogans as "Things go better with..." With enough repetition, even resisted imprints can become part of your inner mind attitudes, and you may follow the path of least resistance and buy the product.

I once had a woman client whose life had been changed for the worse by a major imprint she gave herself when she was five years old. She was of Japanese descent, and grew up in Southern California. She was sixty at the time I worked with her. She had never married and had always pined for a husband. She knew she had some inner block causing her to stay single.

When we checked her inner mind, we found one imprint that was causing this program. When she was five years old her older brother, who was six and a half, tried to have sex with her. (Precocious). She broke and ran away from him and as she ran, he yelled after her, "If you ever get married, you have to do that!" And she responded angrily, "Then, I will never marry!"

She grew up, went to college, and had affairs (only with safely married men). She dated a bachelor for ten years and when he finally asked her to marry him, she told me it was as if a wall came up around her. She couldn't answer him. She said he finally got tired of asking and drifted away. So her life was ruled by one powerful imprint from early childhood until she came to see me. She did release it. Starting at sixty was probably a little late for her but she was happy to be free to accept her life's desire.

If something is strongly communicated to you as a child by an authority figure like a parent, a teacher, or doctor, (or by a peer to a teenager), an imprint may be created with only one statement. If you say something to *yourself* with strong enough emotion, again, it may only take once.

Next is the **Benefit**. We learn about benefits early in life.

As a child, if we scrape our knee, Mom picks us up, kisses it and makes us feel better, giving us love and attention. As we continue through life, we may manipulate others and ourselves to continue to produce these inner mind payoffs.

As we get older, we learn that if we get sick, we get to stay home from school. In our more mature experience, we get to stay home from work. They even call it *benefits* in the work place. How much can we be sick, go to the hospital, stay home?

One of my clients, after I had explained the keys, said, "I recognize all these ways, but especially the benefit. I was raised by Russian Jewish immigrant parents, and I was one of nine children. The only time my mother ever touched me was if I was sick." So, since he was number four of the nine, and also probably had greater need than some of the others, he became the *sick* child.

The poor harassed mother had no time to give to each child unless it was demanded. "But, " he continued, "when I was sick, she was wonderful, she would hold her hand on my forehead all night long!" You could just see this little boy feeling that he surely was in heaven with all that attention. By the way, the man was 72 years old when I worked with him and he related it as if it were yesterday.

Next, we have **Self-Punishment**. We're all *pros* at this one, but you can be especially good at it if you were raised in a Jewish, Catholic, or any Fundamentalist faith.

If you are Jewish, you may have been raised with what I call *a Jewish mother environment*, in other words, often *Great Guilt*. Such guilt may arise from fear of hurting Mother's feelings, not performing, not being what you should be, or not doing what you should do.

The Jewish boy should be a scholar, a success, a professional person. If your talents don't lie in that direction or you've goofed off, you are forever guilty of letting your mother down and you don't deserve a decent life. Generally, with that programming, your inner mind will make sure you'll never have a decent life, either. You may look successful to the outer world, but in your own inner world you'll never measure up.

I had one financially very successful Jewish client whose mother had told him as a child (when he was in a violin recital), "I won't even go if you're not going to be the best." This was regardless of the fact that he was three or four years younger than the top-performing violinist. He had hardly any experience of unconditional love and had trouble showing it to those he loved in later life.

The Catholics have some great traditions, such as confession, and forgiveness of guilt, which help their congregations. There are problems however, when a Christian identifies with the *suffering* of Jesus rather than the forgiveness.

One client, raised in a Catholic grade school, had taken the path of suffering from the second grade. He would pinch himself and hurt himself in different ways in order to be worthy of acceptance by his nun teachers.

Another client was raised in a Catholic convent in South America. She and other girls would eat chalk to become sick with a fever, or put stones in their shoes to suffer the pain that would make them worthy of love and forgiveness.

The main point to remember with Self-Punishment is that it is centered in your belief about what deserves punishment, and what kind of punishment will do that job best. Are you getting enough punishment in the outer world, or do you need to provide it yourself?

You may consciously think you are not punishing yourself in any way. Think again. It's all too likely you have *put yourself* into some position to be blocked or limited in some way.

Next, we have **Conflict**. This is one we are all familiar with. It's that 'twixt and 'tween feeling we get when we're somehow caught in the middle. The simplest way to remember conflict is to know that conflict always has two sides to it.

It's back to fight or flight, and not being able to do either one. If you can take action, fight, move forward, run, surrender, or move away, you'll no longer be in conflict.

Tests on policemen's stress have shown that the officer on the beat is less stressed than the one who is behind a desk. If you think about it you'll see why. Which one is able to use the abilities and skills he's been trained to use? Which is usually kept from making use of those skills? The seeming peacefulness of being behind the desk is offset by the frustration of not being able to take action when challenged, and the lack of resolution that comes with shuffling papers.

You can keep yourself from much happiness and success with inner conflict. Remember all the advice in goal setting. Be clear about what you want, visualize it, then keep focused to produce it in your life.

In other words, be one-pointed. One-pointed, of course, by definition, cannot be two-pointed! An old Russian proverb tells us. "He who chases two rabbits catches neither."

**Organ Language** is the next category. This is rather like an imprint in that it is the result of something you have said to yourself. With Organ Language, however, you actually manifest the statement in your body, or in your life in some way. It can be surprisingly and precisely physical.

For instance, if you have regularly told yourself, "He gives me a headache," or "He's a real pain in the neck, or the tail," you may actually get the headache, or the pain in the neck. You may have lower back pain, or hemorrhoids. Frequently saying, "This makes me sick to my stomach," may bring ulcers, colon problems or other "gut reactions."

Two of our male clients unconsciously created the emotional preconditions that produced massive heart attacks by saying "It's breaking my heart." One of them was a Southerner and staunch Baptist who was very upset by his grown daughter's behavior of living with a man without being married. He kept telling himself she was simply "breaking his heart."

The other man, an airline executive, had no history of heart trouble until his son died two years before in a mountain climbing accident. Ever since, he had been "heart broken" about it, finally expressing that feeling with a near-fatal attack.

Another of my clients shot himself in the foot, unconsciously expressing his conviction that he "couldn't stand" something in his life. Others with coughs, congestion, and allergies expressed their feelings of being "choked up," or "smothered." Sometimes watering eyes or a cold is simply an expression of an inner mind need to cry.

If you get nothing else from this book, I hope you will become more aware of what you are telling yourself, and of the potentially harmful impact of the words of people around you. Don't say "It's driving me crazy," and don't say "It's killing me."

Remember, your inner mind is always listening and is your *genie in the bottle* awaiting your command, mistaken or not.

I had one very clever client in Atlanta come up with the statement, "It's driving me *rich.*" She always had money.

**Experience** is simply what you have gone through for some amount of time. This is different from an imprint in that an imprint is an impression you have perceived. It may be an experience you went through as a child, or in school, in the armed services, or other training. This key focuses on your response to what you have *gone through*, versus what you have seen or heard.

The experience of a childhood with a single parent, having to struggle for the simplest pleasures, or even work as a child to survive, is radically different from the experience of a child of middle class parents, always secure, with no real worries other than who has the latest clothes, or what date to get for the prom.

**Trauma** is actually a breakout of the experience category. A trauma is the result of a single, high impact, negative or fearful experience. It may be powerful enough to suppress completely all conscious recall of an event. A beating or a rape qualify. Someone yelling at you, however, may also qualify if you're a child, or if that someone is perceived to have some real power over you, your life or someone or something you care for.

Trauma is subjective, as are all the keys. The meaning is unique to your inner mind, or your interpretation. It can be traumatic if you perceive it as deeply unacceptable or harmful.

One unusual trauma was experienced by a client of Clark's. The client was a salesman in California, born and raised in Iraq. He had a high percentage of fear of being unpopular. They traced the fear to a major trauma when he was three years old. He mused for a moment, then said, "I know! That was when I burned the house down!"

His family was Christian, and was persecuted in Iraq for it. Several extra family members were living with them. All our client could recall of the incident was that he remembered sitting n the curb, holding his stuffed animal in one hand, and the candle he had started the fire with in the other hand. He was crying not because of the fire, but because he was frightened by the firemen and the commotion. Having forced his entire family onto the streets of Baghdad, he became very unpopular. This justifiably traumatic experience caused the later insecurity.

The last category is **Past Lives.** This is an area I don't like to bring up, but it often comes up anyway in inner mind research with a client. In searching the mind for the reasons for a particular problem, I used to range questions between various ages of the person, to locate the time in life of the experience.

The client's inner mind would sometimes report that the trigger event did not take place in this life, so I would ask, "Is it when you were in the womb?" The answer would be "no," and I would be forced to ask, "Is it something you perceived before that time?" With the yes, I would finally be forced to ask, "Is it from a life you have lived previous to this one?" Then, whether or not the individual had any conscious belief in former lives, it would appear that the inner mind held the belief.

When this occurs, we must handle the belief. For the therapeutic effect, it doesn't really matter whether the belief is true or not. You must let go of *whatever* perception or inner belief is causing the problem.

Often people get very excited over finding inner mind beliefs about past lives, and I am quick to caution them not to get swept away. This life is the one you have to deal with *now*, and all spiritual and religious teachings emphasize this truth.

If you are busily studying supposed past existences, you can be caught up in those stories, and the choices you may or may not have previously made, instead of coping with the challenges in your current life. "Sufficient unto the day is the evil thereof," or we could say, "Sufficient unto the lifetime."

In general, though, we seldom find here-and-now difficulties stemming from a past life reason alone. You have plenty of beliefs, perceptions and judgments in this life to give you enough challenges to work on. In our clinical practice, of course, we are pragmatic and will use *whatever works.*

One of our former students started using "other dimensions" as a category on his own, and found himself multiplying out into people having lives on other planets and in other dimensions after reading of the Richard Bach and Jane Roberts concepts. He felt he was experiencing other probabilities of Self, as well as dealing with"Entities" (something like ghosts that inhabit the same space as the living person) in his life.

These kinds of ideas can come up when you open yourself up to someone with those beliefs. You can imprint yourself, remember, even with a book. As you open yourself to another person, you can pick up his or her beliefs without any conscious intent.If it is a therapist, he can then lead himself right down the path and over the edge with you. The problem is that the therapist will be paid for his time, and you may go home with some new negative or unuseful programming for your money.

The point to remember is this: What is the impact of the

beliefs in your life? Personally I'm open to the possibility that we may be living other lives at the same time as this one, including past and future ones, since there may be no such thing as time outside of this dimension.

We can cause a real problem, however, by getting fascinated by, or addicted to, another dimension of existence, even if it's heavenly. Whatever the merits of such possibilities, I think it's clear that we don't need this kind of distraction that can keep us from learning lessons here.

My husband and I are always aware that whenever we are working with the inner mind of another person, we are really engaged in a kind of hypnosis. Even when you are completely conscious in any kind of therapy, you are open to suggestion. We are incredibly connected in consciousness with you as a client and are aware of this at all times, so that, as the healing admonition says, we "do no harm."

Enough cautions, let's see what you can accomplish now with what we have learned from Response Therapy and how your mind works. I teach my clients to use *The Releasing Strategy* in their daily lives to get in control of their responses. There was a funny comment from one just recently who said she was doing great with it (formerly full of tension, and thinking of leaving her job). She said, "You know, this is really funny, I feel like my brain is being drained... in a positive way, lighter, happier, everything is easier and nothing really bothers me like it used to."

Let's see what we can do towards having that happen for you on your own with this book!

## Chapter 4

# Releasing Your Parents

If you come to us as a client in our private practice, one of the first things we will go after at the inner mind level is the total percentage of positive and negative feelings you have about your mother, your father, and your parents' relationship as you have perceived it. We call this type of information the *Mindmap*™.

Many times the percentages we get are surprising to you. Remember, these measurements are not from your conscious mind. You might have 65% positive feelings about your mother, and 85% negative on her. The two figures are totally separate.

We define them this way. On the positive scale, 100 is unconditional love, and 0 is indifference. On the negative scale, 100 is "cut them up and feed them to the sharks" or as bad as you can feel about anyone, and 0 again is indifference. The numbers in between give the spread of emotion.

I want to focus first on parents since feelings about them form the foundation of our beliefs in the inner mind. You were busily making judgments about them from day one, and your life is predicated on these beliefs, for good or ill. Your parents are at the very least the biological roots you have come from, and if they are not *okay*, where does that leave you?

A simple and direct way to find out what is affecting your life from your parents is to ask yourself, "What was *wrong* with my mother, my father, or their relationship?" Write these negative opinions down, and then, go through them and release them one after the other. Try these examples:

**Releasing On Mother**

**I release my belief, perception, and judgment that ...**

... my mother didn't love me as much as _______________.

... my mother didn't want me to be born.

... my mother wasn't always there for me when I was growing up.

... my mother wasn't nurturing enough to me when I was growing up.

... my mother ever thought I wasn't good enough.

... my mother thought I was ugly.

... my mother thought I was stupid.

... my mother thought I didn't matter.

**I release all fear that ...**

... my mother didn't love me.

(Look to your mind's history to fill in on your individual Releases.) And finally:

**I release my belief, perception, and judgment that ...**

... my mother should have been any different than she was.

... my mother could have been different than she was.

... my mother should be any different than she is now.

The more you are certain that the negative judgment is true, she did hate you, was mean to you, didn't care about you, *the more important it is to release that belief.* Remember, it is just that, a belief. You have no way to go back in time and get into your mother's or anyone else's head. You have no way to know the pressures or programming she was responding to from her own individual perceptions of her childhood or life. You were making these judgments always from a very limited subjective perspective.

The bottom line, I must admit, is simply forgiveness. We must forgive ourselves and everyone else that means or meant anything to us to the point where there is no longer anything to forgive if we are ever to have peace. It is as simple as that. As *A Course In Miracles* puts it, "Would you rather be right, or happy?"

**Releasing On Father**

**I release my belief, perception, and judgment that ...**

... my father loved __________ more than he loved me.

... my father didn't really want me to be born.

... my father didn't care about me.

... my father wasn't nurturing enough to me.

**I release all need or desire to ...**

... punish my father for his shortcomings.

**I release all fear ...**

... my father didn't really love me.

... of my father.

**I release my belief, perception, and judgment that ...**

... my father meant to be so critical.

... I should be critical because my father was critical.

... my father shouldn't have been so fearful or weak.

... my father should have been any different than he was.

... my father wasn't the "perfect" father *for me.*

Remember it is most important to get rid of these negative perceptions especially if they were *true!* It is not for your parent that you need to do this. It is the only way you can be free of that negative reality and be free to create a happy one now.

In the premier of the TV show *Star Trek: Deep Space Nine*, the advanced noncorporeal aliens striving to understand human consciousness, ask the captain, "Why do you choose to live here?" referring to his constant reliving of his horrible memory of his wife's violent death. So, I will ask the same. Why would you choose to keep negative judgments about your history? Why would you choose to live there?

**I release all unwillingness ...**

... to let go of my negative feelings about my father.

**I release all fear ...**

... of loving my father just the way he was or is now.

... my father doesn't love me.

### Releasing Their Relationship

Your parents' relationship gives you your first, often only, and certainly the most important experiential instruction in how to create a mate relationship. Since all of us were born of parents, whether those parents stayed around or not, you have made major judgments on relationships from their example or lack of example. You have had some model of parents in your life. You have in your inner mind a pattern of judgment on that first relationship whether or not you consciously remember your parents at all. The point is that it doesn't matter what the "facts" were, it matters what was judged by you to be the facts. Use *The Releasing Strategy* to help you create their relationship the way it *should have been*.

**I release my belief, perception, and judgment that** ...

... my parents' relationship was never a happy one.

... my parents should never have gotten together.

... my parents didn't love each other in their own way.

... my father ever meant to hurt my mother.

... my father beat my mother.

... my mother ever meant to hurt my father.

... my mother emasculated my father.

... I have to have a relationship like any negative parts of my parents' relationship.

... my father betrayed my mother.

... my mother betrayed my father.

... I would have made a better mate for my father/mother than my mother/father.

... my parents should have given me a better example of a mate relationship.

**I release all unwillingness ...**

... to accept my parents' relationship just the way it was.

... to forgive my parents their relationship.

**I release all fear that...**

... I have to have an unhappy mate relationship because of my parents' relationship.

**I release my belief, perception, and judgment that**...

... my parents' relationship wasn't perfect for them.

... my parent's relationship should have been what I would choose for myself now.

After Releasing the negative judgments about your biological parents, you must do the same for all the parental figures you have had in your life. If you had a stepparent, or other parental substitute who was instrumental in raising you, you must clean up those judgments. Also, release any on stepparental relationships as you perceived them.

These Releasing Processes on parents, parental figures, and their relationships are the most important cleansing processes you can ever do for your peace of mind, and to create a happy life for yourself now and in the future.

## Chapter 5

# Freeing Yourself and Your Childhood

If you didn't have perfect parents, there's a fair chance you didn't have a perfect childhood either. Also, you just might have made some critical judgments about yourself along the way that aren't doing you any good today.

What's wrong with you? You are the one who knows, and may try to keep it out of your mind. You may distract yourself from that awful truth, or possibly truths.

These supposed truths are probably about how limited you are, and certainly not as good as other people, or as clever, or as deserving in any way. If you did deserve your good, you would surely be rich, or famous, or at least have more of that *happiness* stuff in your life. Things would work for you, instead of your feeling you're an example of Murphy's Law. People would care about you, and you would be more rewarded for your efforts in life.

Let's see if we can make a dent in this. Read aloud...

**I release my belief, perception, and judgment that** ...

... I wasn't as good as I should have been as a child.

... I should have been perfect, or should be now.

... I should have been smarter in school.

... I should have achieved more.

**I release my belief, perception, and judgment that…**

… I should have made more friends.

… I shouldn't have had sex when I did.

… I should have had sex when I didn't.

… I should be thinner/fatter than I am.

… I won't be able to get my body into the shape I want.

… I'm not good enough just the way I am.

… I'm not lovable, or worth loving.

… I don't deserve to get what I want.

… I need to feel guilty about anything in my life.

…. no one will ever love me.

… I'm not creative.

… I'm not clever.

… I'm not good looking.

… I'm not as spiritual as other people.

… I should be any different than I really am.

… I don't deserve to be forgiven.

… I don't deserve love.

… I shouldn't have been born to the family I was.

… I'm not good enough for my family.

… my family never wanted me.

… I didn't deserve the good I've received in life.

… I don't deserve my good now.

As you can see, we can go on and on. You may have some of

these beliefs, and assuredly you will have inner assumptions that are uniquely yours. Create your own Releasing Statements now on what was wrong with your childhood, and on what was wrong, or is wrong with you.

**I release all fear ...**

... of Releasing my negative thoughts about myself.

**I release my belief, perception, and judgment that ...**

... I don't deserve to be free of negative beliefs about myself.

Your negative beliefs and fears about yourself can come up and run your life at any time if they're allowed to get rooted in your inner mind. Since we're not taught as children to release, or to let go of unhelpful beliefs, we generally have a fair quantity built up by the time we are adults. You have to *want* to transform your life into something else. You have to *want* a better life!

Let's create a second childhood, have it the way it should have been. You can do it. You simply use *The Releasing Strategy* just as we have been demonstrating. Release on each thing that should have been different. Then, consciously add in the beliefs you should have had enter your inner mind if you and your parents could have known how.

Now I want you to experience a special series I developed when I worked with a young woman in Atlanta. She had been very close to her father when she was a child. She had fond memories of his taking her along with him as he farmed their land. She was always with him and he was very partial to her and loving until she turned eleven and puberty occurred.

Suddenly, he turned cold, and wouldn't touch her or give her any affection. Her life since that time had been plagued by a poor self-image, and as an adult, she found herself always trying to please a mate who, like her father, wouldn't give her affection or attention. Even her realizing from an adult perspective that he probably was afraid of becoming sexually attracted to a daughter he loved, didn't heal the lack of expressed affection in those formative years. So, I decided to use *The Releasing Strategy* to help her reframe those years of lost affection that she needed.

You can do it too! First, for your mother, and the relationship you should have had, say aloud:

**I release my belief, perception, and judgment** that ...

... my mother didn't hold me, and hug me and love me every day until I was *five.*

... my mother didn't hold me, and hug me and love me every day until I was *ten.*

... my mother didn't hold me, and hug me and love me every day until I was *fifteen.*

... my mother didn't hold me, and hug me and love me every day until I was *twenty.*

... my mother isn't *always* there *now* to hold me, and hug me and love me whenever I need her to.

Note any resistance you have to saying these Releases. It is very important to say each one, let me repeat, even or especially if your mother didn't do this. She may have died, or been out of your life for one reason or another. Remember, you are saying these Releases *for you,* and for the positive emotional foundation you need to create.

And now for your father.

**I release my belief, perception, and judgment that ...**

... my father didn't hold me, and hug me and love me, every day until I was *five.*

... my father didn't hold me, and hug me and love me every day until I was *ten.*

... my father didn't hold me, and hug me and love me every day until I was *fifteen.*

... my father didn't hold me, and hug me and love me every day until I was *twenty.*

... my father isn't *always* there *now* to hold me, and hug me and love me whenever I need him to.

Remember, it's especially important to do these Releases if your parents were cold, unloving, "never there," or seemed to act as if they didn't care about you.

As you will see when you try to say them, these particular Releases have an incredible amount of power. I've had people going along smoothly until we got into these, and then had them choke up, go into tears, or not be able to say the statements.

You see, when something very important and really necessary for your emotional growth is missing, it's like you're missing a vertebra from your emotional structure. You will grow lopsided and never even realize how heavily you are compensating all your life.

So, go on. Make it the way it should have been. It won't make your conscious memory all that different. You will still remember the *bad stuff* when you want. The strange thing is, you won't have the pain when you think about those things. In other words, you won't have the buttons to get pushed anymore.

This chapter, and the previous one on your parents, point to the most important work you can do for yourself. These areas – your parents, their relationship, and you and your childhood – are where it all began. Their influences continue until you change them.

So do it! Be thorough. Remember, if you miss something, you can always get it again. It only takes a few seconds to let it go using *The Releasing Strategy*.

Chapter 6

# Consciously Creating Your Mate Relationship

You and your mate, or prospective mate, come to your relationship with a full complement of inner assumptions from your perceptions about your parents, and their relationship, your past love relationships of various kinds, and all the male/female relationships you have seen, read about or experienced in any way. That's a heavy load! No wonder so many relationships flounder when there is any added stress, or after the honeymoon is over.

With this understanding, you must empty your inner mind of negative perceptions you are carrying about any of those former relationships or people.

Again, you will have your own list of things to release and reasons to do it. Here are some examples to work with.

**I release my belief, perception, and judgment that ...**
...my first/or former lover shouldn't have been so jealous.
...______________ meant to hurt me in any way.
...any other mate will leave me because ___________ left me.
...I can't trust men/women because of my experience with ______________.
...my first or former love should still be with me, or married to me.
... I should have married _________________.
... I shouldn't have married _________________.
...s/he shouldn't have fallen in love with or married someone else.

**I release my belief, perception and judgment that…**

…s/he should have left his/her other mate for me.

…I should have had his baby.

…I shouldn't have had his baby.

…s/he should have had a baby with me.

…s/he shouldn't have had a baby with me.

…I won't have a better mate for me.

…any current or future mate will be critical of me because ______________ was.

…I'm guilty for leaving ______________.

…I can't be free in a relationship now because I felt trapped in that one.

**I release all fear**…

…that I can't have a happy mate relationship now because of any former relationship.

…of men/women because of my fears about ____________.

**I completely release** …

… ______________ from all obligation to me now.

… myself from all obligation to ______________ .

**I release my belief, perception, and judgment that** …

… my former relationship should have been any different than it was.

… I can't have a happy intimate relationship because of my former relationship.

… the relationship wasn't a useful learning experience for me.

… I'm not stronger and better off now because I had that (those) relationship(s).

If you have been keeping yourself from forming any current attachments because of the past experiences you have had with love relationships, maybe it's time now to change that. Why not give it a try? What have you got to lose? You may lose some unhappiness. You can live a very safe life never getting intimately involved with another person. You can also end up feeling very useless and unfulfilled.

One man I worked with was very much in love with a woman. They had dated for a number of years, and had even tried living together for a few months but she and her young son had moved out as he seemed so inflexible and controlling. He was 42 and had never been married, seemingly because he could never commit to one woman. He had a lot of girlfriends, one for every occasion. He was very successful financially, and so, on the surface, he seemed rather like a spoiled child. He came to me desperate. She was considering another man, and my client realized he was about to lose her.

He seemed on the surface to be just a selfish person who wanted a mate with no commitment on his part. However, at the base of his emotions and reactions was a mass of judgments especially about his father. One was an imprint from his childhood. His mother had always cautioned him and his brothers to "be quiet so you won't disturb your father."

His father had been an overweight drinker and smoker and literally dropped dead with a heart attack in front of the boy. From that experience, he took on not only guilt for his father's death, but the inner belief that *children's noise could kill.* This also meant, therefore, that children's noise could kill him! This was the overriding inner assumption that held him from creating an environment that would allow children - i.e. marriage. And remember, the woman he wanted had a young child.

The other basis for why he could not marry was misguided loyalty to a former girlfriend. She had been his best friend for twenty years but was never really a sexual interest. There was no "chemistry" for him. They had similar intellectual interests, and were very active in the same sport. Most important was the fact that she had nursed him back to health after his leg was terribly injured in an accident. She was also content to "wait for him" through all his interests in other women.

This loyalty to his friend was ruining his chances for creating the relationship he really wanted. It was also ruining his former girlfriend's prospects of having a real relationship with anyone else.

So, everyone was stuck. Using *The Releasing Strategy*, I was able to help him free himself from his formerly glued position. His prospective wife also went through the process, and they were married a few months later. They couldn't be happier, and he's a great daddy to the little boy.

The case just described occurred five years ago and I was very pleased to get a referral of another couple this summer from the wife. The new client called me and asked us to work with her and her husband, because her friend said "we had transformed their relationship."

I was, of course, thrilled to hear the work we had done was still effective for them. We have many cases of real turnarounds with The Cameron Method, using *The Releasing Strategy*, but we don't always get to hear about them after this much time. Most former clients are busy off living their lives and it just doesn't cross people's minds to call and say, "It's still working!"

Ruth was a wife of a corporate executive. She was also a talented dancer who had a career dancing and teaching dance. She came to me depressed, and close to leaving her husband whom she saw as cold, distant and not really understanding of her life and of her passionate nature.

She had had a secret love interest, a man who was in her profession, for several years. It was not a sexual relationship - yet. As she became more dissatisfied with her husband, the sexual involvement was becoming more probable. With her ethical and religious convictions, if she did get involved sexually, she would have to leave her husband.

Ruth was a quick student, who was willing to let go of the negative judgments about her husband (as well as everyone else in her life). Her comments later were typical of what we hear from clients. "I don't know how, or why, but *he's* different." No longer the trapped wife, she was able to enjoy her marriage, and let go of her need for the other man.

One last thought about mate relationships. There is a common belief that they are only important to women. True, I saw the *Cathy* comic strip that had Cathy reading all the relationship books, while Irving her boyfriend sat next to her reading his *Hot Rod* magazines. Well, men may not *act* as "interested," but they *need* the relationship just as much if not more.

Studies have shown men don't live as long without a mate. There is no real or long term satisfaction in revolving mate relationships for men or women. There are also the very real health concerns of AIDS, and other genital diseases. I'm not overlooking the *Playboy Magazine* version of a typical man's ideal sex life. Even Hugh Heffner, who realized the ultimate male lifestyle fantasy, called marriage and family "the natural next step" for him.

In business, employers are always happier if the higher echelon person is *settled* in a relationship. If that relationship or marriage is having problems, it can scuttle the best job capabilities.

With *The Releasing Strategy*, you can sculpt the relationship you consciously want. You can be free from those old negative hooks and inner clamps in your love life. It's simply up to you. Is there anything in your relationship/s that should be or should have been different?

If so, you have the power and the tool to clean it out!

## Chapter 7

# Sex: What It's Really All About

Sex is such an important area of life that there are uncountable numbers of books on the subject cataloging all the feelings and foibles that go with it.

I want to get into an area here that is seldom acknowledged in books and theories on sex and sexual relationships. I want to explain the differences between men and women. Well, I know what you're thinking. You learned all that a long time ago... What I'm talking about is the different ways that men and women view sex, and sexual relationships. Not only do we, as humans, have experiential emotional programming on the subject, we also have biological mindsets that are seldom accepted, honored or even consciously recognized.

There have been many relationship books such as *Women Who Love Too Much, Smart Women Foolish Choices, The Cinderella Complex*, etc. There's nothing really wrong with them. The authors are sincere, and are trying to help women to avoid a negative life. Misery, however, loves company and righteousness increases as we let an author reinforce our belief that we were the victim of a man who did us wrong, poor us!

When these victim books have recognized the reality of our pain, we may gather in support groups to reinforce the teachings and beliefs of the authors. Too often, however, this support only reinforces the existing painful perceptions and memories.

It would be so nice if, by being *careful* or even by abstaining, we could avoid ever again being hurt. Relationship programming is not really the same as addiction to drugs or alcohol. There is emotional addictive programming to be sure, but I believe it is reinforcing that programming to sit in a group and confess that "I have screwed up, trusted the wrong mate, picked the wrong mate, and have even done it more than once!"

Instead of holding an AA or Alanon-type meeting as though you have an incurable addiction to poor mate choices, let's do something useful about the mindset that's creating the problems.

First, let's look at some of the real differences between men and women. There has been a lot of complaining from women about men such as: "Men are insensitive clods," "Men are sex crazy, and all they ever think about is sex."

You may feel he wouldn't be attracted to other women if he really loved you (instead of noticing everything that moves in a skirt on the street). If he really respected you, he wouldn't talk about how sexy, attractive, or what a *come-on* other women are. He must be trying to tell you you're not enough! He doesn't care for you the way he should.

The complaint from men is, "I don't want to be just a meal ticket." "I want a woman who is independent (doesn't need my money), but I don't want her to have control in the relationship." "Why can't I find a woman who wants sex as much as I do?" "Where is a woman who will accept me the way I am?" "I want a woman I can really please, who won't want to change me all the time."

Let's go back to where this programming may be rooted. Let's go back to primitive society.That's where our hormones still are, and they're more influential than any of us like to admit. Let's pretend that the inner psyche may still be back in the cave mentality.

In the cave, a woman would not be criticized for choosing a powerful mate. As the physically more vulnerable of the sexes, you would need that power to protect you and provide for the biological continuation of the race, the children.

In modern society, as a woman, you still have the responsibility for bearing, and usually for rearing the children, but you also may have to play the role of providing the protection and sustenance. In other words, you should have a good job, or money of your own so you don't put too much pressure on the man to provide.

Ah, back to dowries! But let's have equality. That has come to mean, for the poor feminists, that you should be able to *do it all,* as well as have it all. You should just want your mate for companionship and, of course, you should *always* be ready and interested in sex.

I have another bit of bad news. Women as a group do *not* have the same sex drive as men. Let's look at the biology again, and race continuation. A woman can only physically produce maybe fifteen to twenty children in a lifetime. That's if you start young and don't do much else with your life. You'd also be pretty worn out, I think.

Men, however, can provide their precious sperm to a thousand women, and most men would love to volunteer for the duty. (Could that be why men love war so? Does each think he will be the survivor who gets to perform the reproductive rites in behalf of his fallen comrades?)

This all goes along with the fact that you men as a group with your testosterone, get yourselves into wars, fights, grand efforts, stress, conflicts, and in general kill yourselves off a lot faster and sooner than women. You can often really feel underneath it all that you're very replaceable.

Here's another interesting thought to consider. If you are a woman, you are connected to immortality by your ability to bear children. You never have to do it, just know that it is possible. You never have to worry *what* you will *be* when you grow up. Not really. You know you can be a mother, a truly powerful role. The hand that rocks the cradle does rule at least that cradled individual's world. What could be more powerful than participating in the creation and continuation of life!

I suggest the truth is just the opposite of Freud's penis envy. The boy child, when he is born, finds himself cared for by a powerful being. She runs his whole world. She even feeds him from her breast. The most hopeful thing this tiny soul can think is, "When I grow up, I will be powerful and strong like this person, Mommy." Then, somewhere along the way, he finds out that he can't be a mommy. His Superbeing is out. He has to be like that other person, the one he hasn't seen much because the father may have been away earning a living, or away from the child for some other reason. The boy can then decide, well, if he can't be like Mommy, he can at least marry her. Whoops, wrong again. That daddy person or some other powerful male already has her.

So, there he goes, for all his life, looking to express the power he felt so little of for so many critical years. He puts his name on "his" children. In the hope that they are, in fact, his children.

As a man, you may also put your name on your business, in

an effort to have something of yourself live after you. Your business or career, therefore, becomes your creation in the world. No wonder you can devote so much of yourself to it, often to the exclusion or neglect of your family.

Think about it. A woman never has to wonder *"Who's child is it?"* She knows it's hers. The poor man, however, could be investing in raising another man's gene pool. (Horror). So he, at least, wants to put his name on the child as a statement that this investment is his, and to announce to the rest of the world that the child and woman are under his protection and provision. This claimstake need of the male has been useful for both sexes.

As to sexual stimulation, the male, because of the need to be able to replant the race, is indiscriminately susceptible to a myriad of stimuli. He can be visually *set off* by a simple curve of a buttocks, a wave of long hair, or a bosomy jiggle of the right configuration. He really can't help it, and when he wants to share his feelings with his mate, she takes offense! So most men try to hide their feelings about this. They will only share it if they feel safe, which is usually with other men who have the same reactions.

When I have told male clients of the studies that find men think about sex about every thirty seconds, they're never surprised. Women almost always are.

Finally, I tell women, no wonder men are so easily stimulated. Just think how hard it must be, to have your genitals hanging out like that, open to being bumped against, or knowing they have a will of their own, and are apt to be set off at any inopportune time or place.

So, men have the problem of identity, and who will ever

know they have lived, and who will care? The need for power goes with the problem, and the need to perform. They need to perform to attract or deserve the best mate. They want the mate as Warren Farrell describes in his book, *Why Men Are The Way They Are,* who has the "*beauty genes*."

As a man, your identity often centers in performance. Who you are, is defined by what you do or the power you command in the world. If you are a woman, on the other hand, you can choose to express yourself in different ways. There is not the *innate* need to perform in the outer world to deserve a mate. Your need to perform comes from the real need to support yourself economically, but not for your emotional satisfaction or identity. Problems may come for you, however, in the conflict of your conscious desire for outer world performance or a career, and your inner desire to nest or have a family.

Many a female client of mine, when we have gotten to the inner level of what she really wanted in life, has been consciously surprised to find that, underneath it all, she really wanted to be married and have a child.

My husband, Clark, in the early nineteen seventies, on the University of California at Berkeley campus, that marvelous hotbed of feminism, took an inner mind survey of what women on campus really wanted in a career. He was fully expecting to help with career choices.

What he found with the subconscious questioning, to the surprise and disgust of many of the women being questioned, was that most really wanted to get married and have babies. Men aren't the only ones with problems!

This basis of the cave, or biological programming, underlies many of the conflicts women have over their mate choices, and what they're up to in the world. The need to have a powerful mate comes into early manifestation as being attracted to the tall (big), or powerful body.

This is soon overcome by the unconscious recognition of where the real power in this world is. Power is in what controls other people or provides protection or support. What produces money usually does the trick. That's why surveys show that a woman is less concerned with schooling in a mate, than with his ability to earn a good living. You can forgive a lot if your mate provides the best care for you and your children.

I think the earning capacity of a man usually has a great deal to do with how much *nagging* his wife will do. She usually will not be so critical of his foibles if they do not threaten her situation. If he gambles, or is less than the perfect mate, it's often all right if it doesn't threaten the home and hearth.

One of my clients told me her mate had just sheepishly confessed, after a weekend at Lake Tahoe gambling, that he had lost $10,000. They have a very nice home, he has an expensive sports car, and she has her own very good job, so it was only a fairly minor irritation to her. She told him that she guessed he really *learned something* on that trip. To most of us, it would be "Katy bar the door"!

Another one told me an interesting story of visiting her sister and the sister's multimillionaire husband. The client said the husband was belching very ungraciously at the table, with never so much as a "pardon me." When she said something to her sister about it later, the sister excused him saying, "When a man has the money to buy and sell people, he doesn't need manners." These are certainly not the usual experiences for most of us. (One note on this couple: the wife did finally divorce him after 20 years of marriage, and she didn't have to give up her lifestyle. He had the power to buy and sell people, but not keep his wife.)

When you as a woman are complaining, or seem to be nagging your mate, you are coming from a fear that maybe you have chosen wrongly. Maybe you feel trapped because you have had children, or have committed yourself to this mate, and here he is, not the Prince Charming, or the powerful person you thought he was.

If he won't take care of you and the children the way he should, or he promised, then you may be out on the street looking for another, and will definitely find it a harder sell because you have the children along.

So, the reasoning is, maybe you can fix up the fellow you have. If he would just listen to you, he could become the prince you thought he was all the time. It's always logical, yet for *some reason*, the man almost always takes offense.

Here is the basis for the familiar male complaint, "She wants to change me, and won't accept me the way I am." The more threatened you are, the worse it gets. Remember, nagging comes from feelings of frustration and lack of power. The more he feels attacked, the more he will not trust you and will withdraw from you, thus aggravating your fears again. Round and round we go.

In many relationships, there is also the problem of the division of labor. A Boston University study on housework, reported in *Working Mother Magazine* in an article by Debra Kent, revealed that men do the same minimal amount of it regardless of whether their wives work outside the home or not. Also, single mothers spend less time than married moms do on household tasks, 16 hours, versus 20 hours per week for married women. It suggests that a husband *generates* at least four more hours of housework for a woman than no husband!

As the article by Kent asserts, "It's not news that women are sexually attracted to powerful, take-charge men; arousal is intertwined with respect and admiration. But try getting excited about a guy who can't pick up his dirty socks, scramble an egg or buy his own underwear. It's not easy to respect a man who's whiny and helpless around the house. With this loss of respect often comes a loss of sexual interest."

Anger also dims sexual interest; if you feel taken advantage of, or exploited, sex becomes just one more demand, or job. Remember too, fear is underneath anger, another turn off. Back to what we can do for the inner mind programming. Since all we ever have to handle is fear of one kind or another, let's go after those unuseful ones from the biological side, too. We may not be able to end forever all biologically based fears, but we can at least get them manageable.

First, from the feminine point of view...

**I release my belief, perception, and judgment that my mate ...**

... doesn't love me if he is attracted to other women.
... shouldn't have sexual thoughts about other women, and
... shouldn't want to share those thoughts with me.
... isn't strong enough.
... won't always love me,
... won't be there when I need him.
... should be stronger, isn't getting to be stronger.

... doesn't pay enough attention to my needs.

... should always listen to me.

... isn't perfect for me just the way he is.

... threatens my life or security in any way.

...isn't getting better all the time.

**I release my belief, perception, and judgment that ...**

... I can't count on my mate.

... I can't be patient and loving with my mate if he doesn't perform as I want him to.

... I have to be the only one in charge of household tasks.

**I release my belief, perception, and judgment that...**

... I can't get help from my mate, or hire it done for both of us.

... I chose the wrong mate.

... some other mate is better for me.

And from the *masculine* point of view ...

**I release my belief, perception, and judgment that ...**

... my mate nags me too much.

... she only wants me for my money.

... she won't stop criticizing me.

... she has changed too much after having the children.

... she loves the children more than me.

... she doesn't want sex enough anymore.

... she doesn't take care of her looks enough now.

... she isn't fun anymore.

... I can't accept her just the way she is.

... I can't love her and be patient with her just the way she is.

... things won't get better between us.
... I can't forgive her, start over with her.
... I shouldn't help with household tasks.
... I have to get even with her.

Both sexes: Create your own best Releasing Statements to handle the main issues that arise in your relationship with the opposite sex and use them! This last statement above (about getting even) brings us to the next chapter on Power and Control. Can you have power and control in your life while still having a good and satisfying mate relationship? Let's take a look at that now.

## Chapter 8

# Who's in Charge?

Power and Control. Sounds great, doesn't it? It's what we all want in our lives. Of course we would have happiness if we could just have power and control. "If I ruled the world..."

Ah, that's the trick. If everyone, or that special someone, would only do what I want, only be what I want, then I could be content. If I just had what I want, had security, or the ability to travel where I want in the style or way I want, then I would be content. If people would just leave me alone, or if people would just pay attention to me, I could be content. If I just had the power to make my life the way it should be, I would be content.

I don't want too much. Other people have what I want, so it must not be impossible, it's just that I must be doing something wrong. They have more power than I do. Someone is blocking me or stopping me. God doesn't care about me as much as other people, *I must be powerless.*

Sometime along the way in life, we may learn that the only real power and control that works is the ability to have power and control *over our own selves*. We do have free will. We have the power to make the judgments of what we will think about, and therefore, what we will create in our lives, given the circumstances and resources we command.

We judge what is important, or of meaning, or what is acceptable or unacceptable from other people. No matter what circumstances we find ourselves in, we use this power to be happy or unhappy and depressed, secure or uncertain and insecure, powerful or victimized and "at effect" of events and people.

I am constantly impressed by the variety of my clients' problems. I mean the variety of circumstances that people find produce problems for them. For instance, I have worked with wealthy people with private planes and beautiful homes, who are unable to create a happy mate relationship. Recently, I had one man in this category tell me, "I've always been successful in business and making money but I've never known how to communicate with my mate. My parents never communicated either."

He had been living with his mate for 7 or 8 years but never wanted to marry. He thought she didn't appreciate him or what he was doing for her. She was starting to pull away as he resisted marriage. He said, "What more does she want? I have her in my will to get several hundred thousand." In almost the next breath he said, "She makes me so mad, I think I'll cut her out of my will!" I don't think this is the kind of security a woman wants from her mate!

I have had financially well-off clients who are retired and free to travel and otherwise enjoy life tell me they can't get along because of a drinking problem, lack of communication, disparity in sex drives, or disagreement over investment policies and financial security.

Other clients who have never had a secure job, say that if only they could work for a company like Hewlett Packard, which is known for treating its employees well, they would have it made. Then my very next client may be a Hewlett Packard employee, terribly upset because he feels *stuck* in his job.

I have had people who are without a mate in their life, and feel unhappy over that. One man I worked with was a professional, had a house (in Silicon Valley), and was nice looking. It seemed he could have had his choice of many women. He had been married for a number of years, was divorced and single again for about ten years.

The man was miserable. He could think of nothing but his lack of a mate. He told me he had met and asked out over 60 women in the past six months, and had *struck out* with every one. I even introduced him to another of my former clients, and when nothing came of it, asked her why not? What was he doing wrong? She commented that she understood what he was feeling because that's how she herself, had felt before. He was just too *needy*. He was projecting that feeling out to every woman he met.

There was another problem with this particular man. He set his standards so high, they were always just out of his reach. The woman for him had to meet high physical standards, as well as be independent of him financially. Instead of looking to fill a *woman's* needs on some level, he focused only on his own.

He wasn't a Rockefeller in finances, or an Adonis in physique. He was over 50, and for a woman with a good career of her own, he could be a poor risk. Remember, a woman will instinctively be drawn to the more powerful male. How can he protect her if she is more powerful than he is? If he is older, he'd better be able to balance off the loss of physical power with financial or social power.

He was pining away for the *perfect* woman. Meanwhile, there were many who could have met his desires for sexual compatibility, and companionship. He could get either financial independence, or physical allure, but probably not both. Part of his failure in this department, I feel, was the fact that he would not accept this basic idea. When I explained it to him, he simply said, "I don't believe that."

He might as well have said, "I don't want to believe that." But on an inner level he knew it only too well. He would unerringly pick a woman who would, sooner or later, reject him.

He, himself, was rejecting most women for not meeting his standards, and then getting the mirror reflection from the women he deemed acceptable. So he continued in his efforts to get women who were actually inappropriate, and continued to be miserable.

This brings us back to the Releasing Statement using the words *belief, perception, and judgment.* If you *believe* you can or you can't, you're right. If you *perceive* there is no way out for you to escape your terrible situation, you're right. And, if you *judge* your perception to be true, *for good or ill,* you will be right.

The remarkable document, *A Course In Miracles* asks the question, "Would you rather be right, or happy?" Our egos almost invariably will answer, "Be right!" At least when we stubbornly stick to our unhappy mindset, we feel the power and control of being *right.* It won't give us anything more for all our effort, but if we can't have real power, it feels like a close substitute.

What is important to you? If you feel you can't create it in your life, you will feel a lack of power or control. Simple as that.

Let's see how we can impact this mindset.

**I release my belief, perception, and judgment that I can't feel control and power in my life ...**

... if I don't have more money.

... if I don't have a mate.
... if I can't control the mate I have.
... if my mate doesn't love me anymore.
... if my mate doesn't love me the way s/he should.
... if I don't have my own home.
... if I don't have someone to share my life.
... if people are demanding too much of me.
... if I'm not popular enough.
... if I'm not smart enough.
... if my body isn't as strong as it should be.
... if my body isn't as slim as it should be.
... if my body isn't proportioned as it should be.
... if I'm not as beautiful/handsome as someone else.

**I release all fear...**
...that I can't control my habits.
...that I can't exercise enough.
...that I can't make people like me, or leave me alone.
...that I will lose my health.
...that I won't regain my health.
...that I can't trust God or a higher power in my life.
...that I can't let go!

**I release my belief, perception and judgment ...**
**that I have no power ...**
... if I don't have as much money as someone else has.
... if I don't have as many things as someone else has.
... if I'm not as powerful as someone else.
... if I don't win in every effort.
... if I can't sell everyone I want to on my ideas, or desires.

... if the ozone layer and our environment is being destroyed.
... if we may be the generation that will ruin the planet.

**I release my belief, perception, and judgment that I don't have power...**

... because I should be able to do something about all the misery in the world.

... just the way I am.

**I release all fear ...**

... that I can't make a difference in my world.

The thing to remember in all this is that the power you want is really always there for you. You must only get out of your own way to know it and express it. Releasing is your door to open to the power you want. *Say it even when you feel that it won't make any difference to say it.*

Say it especially if you have a lot of evidence from the outer world to support your view of your impotence. Make yourself use *The Releasing Strategy.* Just take the attitude that you'll say it anyway. It doesn't hurt, and doesn't really take that much time or effort. What have you got to lose? It just might work. It will work, if you use it! It won't if you don't.

## Chapter 9

# How to Stop Hurting

We have dealt with a variety of physical problems and pain in our practice of Response Therapy, and have had a very respectable track record using *The Releasing Strategy*. It doesn't always work to take away all problems, or pain, but then nothing works every time, or for all people.

We are especially happy if the client has had all sorts of medical tests, and the doctors have thrown up their hands. Then we are more assured that the underlying cause or causes of the problem will most probably lie in our area of expertise.

We have had good results with back pain, stomach pains, cramps, headaches, blurred vision, lessening of menstrual cramps, facial ticks, a goiter about to be operated on, warts, lack of sexual orgasm, laryngitis, pain with intercourse, insomnia, impotence, allergies, arthritis, and all kinds of stress reactions.

My client with blurred vision had a particularly interesting problem. She had been to renowned doctors at a prestigious university hospital, had been through extensive testing by neurologists who told her, "We can't find anything wrong with your eyes or your brain. There is some unknown reason that your brain is not getting the message to your eyes to focus!"

This client came in on referral from another client, and we spent a Saturday afternoon (4 hours), uncovering and removing the underlying reasons that were causing her very involved problem.

There were nine inner mind reasons for her blurred or double vision. At root, she was leading a very stressful life. She was married, had three older children, boys, and her last child was a little girl who was now almost two. Her husband was a partner/ manager in a restaurant business, often having to be away 12 or more hours a day, coming home exhausted himself.

She was actively involved in La Leche League, the organization that supports nursing mothers. She believed that a mother should nurse her baby as long as the baby wants it. Generally, that's a fine idea. This particular child, however, was continuing to want to nurse every two hours *day and night.*

The mother's inner mind was rebelling to try to create some rest. Not only was she not getting any full night's sleep, she had an active family to care for besides!

As you can see, it was a logical step for her inner mind to take, and it worked. Well, sort of. She was still getting up every two hours to nurse, but she was wearing an eye patch to drive, and to get around. In this way, she was getting rest, one eye at a time.

Three of the nine reasons for blurred vision were inner mind benefits: first, to get to shut her eyes and rest; second, to excuse herself from having to accept the demands of the children; and third, to get her away from home (while she went to various doctors).

Another reason was Organ Language. She felt she was *in a fog* all the time.

We released on all the reasons and then I questioned the inner mind, "Are you willing to let go of the double vision by next month?" The answer was affirmative. Then I asked, "Within two weeks?" Again affirmative. Then, "A week?," yes, and, "By tomorrow?"

A slower affirmative appeared with each of these questions. Then, "Are you willing to let go of the blurred vision now?" Immediately, "No!" With more Releasing on her fear of letting go of the program, her inner mind agreed to let go of it within an hour. I stopped pressuring it then and went on to look at other things in her inner mind.

About 45 minutes later, she said, "I want to tell you, I've been afraid to believe it myself, but I've been seeing clearly for a while now." It was an extremely moving moment for both of us.

She was able to leave that day seeing for the first time in many months. She had some relapses as she continued her stressful life, but did finally wean her baby. She was able to get control of her stressful programming, and the habit it had become.

So, with physical problems, it is most important to release on *all* the reasons that might be causing it. Then remember to release on the habit, and all fear of being *without* the problem. Remember the saying, "At least it's the devil I know."

Here are some examples:

**I release my belief, perception, and judgment that I should have this pain, or physical problem because ...**

... I deserve to have pain, or this problem.

... my mother/father had pain or a problem like this.

... I told myself I always will have it.

... doctors have told me I have it.

... this pain or problem will get sympathy or attention for me.

... the pain will give me an excuse not to go back to work.

... I should be punished this way, or any way.

... I am in conflict in my love life, career, or family life.
... my body is symbolizing that something is *a pain* for me.
... I have had the experience of having this pain or problem, and I'm used to it.
... of any Past Life reason.

**I release all need or desire...**
... to have pain, or any physical problem in my body.

**I release all fear ...**
... of being without pain.
... of this pain.

Remember, with pain, or other physical problems, you are contending with constant reinforcement of the problem by your physical perceptions. You will be going against all your other senses. It can seem futile and foolish even to be saying the Releasing Statements. Your mind may be thrown into great conflict because of it. Just do it anyway.

Another interesting case of mine, when I was in Atlanta, was a fireman who complained of back pain. He felt he could not let anyone in the department know about his problem because he was afraid he would be out of a job he loved, and he had a family, so he privately went to M.D.s and chiropractors and simply performed with pain most of the time.

We found the inner mind reasons, and released them. Then we worked on the other important issues and people in his life, and cleared up his back problem.

Later, when he came in for a session to work on some other

things, he said he was about to take his family for a vacation skiing. I thought, "Oh great, there goes all our work on his back." I had him release any reasons to tense up his back, or have pain again, and especially any reasons to have any injury on the slope!

I must say that I was relieved and very happy to hear him report when he returned that he had had a great time, with some sore muscles, but no recurrence of back pain or injury. He has continued to remain pain free.

You can do it too!

**I release my belief, perception, and judgment that ...**

... I should have pain because my mother/father had pain.

... my body will react with pain because anyone in my family has had pain or physical problems.

... I should have pain or any physical problem because any one said I should, or will.

... I can't get rid of the pain or physical problem because I wastold I can't.

... I have to die, or be sick because other people have, or I am expected to.

... I get any benefit from having pain or a physical problem.

... I get any useful attention or love because of having pain or a physical problem.

... I need to punish myself for anything by having a pain or a physical problem.

... my physical problem or pain is useful for me to express any guilt.

... I need to have pain or ______________ (physical problem) because of any stress or conflict.

... I can't resolve the conflicts in my life without feeling pain

in my body.
... I have to express the pain in my life or my situation by having pain or physical problems in my body.

**I release my belief, perception, and judgment that...**
... I have to have pain or physical problems because of any trauma in my past.
... I have to have pain or physical problems because I have had them in the past.

**I release all need or desire ...**
**...** to continue to have pain or physical problems for any reason.

Go ahead and put your own Releasing Statements together. They will be more powerful as you are closer to your own history. You can sense where you don't want to let go of something. The more it seems natural to keep it, the better to release it!

## Chapter 10

# You Don't Have To Be Lonely

You are never lonely without a frame of reference for that loneliness. It comes back to the belief that "I should have someone with me, who would understand me, that I could share my life with." You can have it, and I agree with you, you should have it. Why not? You have been creating many things in your life you may not have consciously chosen. You now can consciously choose and produce what you do want!

Somehow, if you are lonely, you have gotten the belief in your inner mind that there is no one for you in this world. As strongly as you believe this, it will continue to be true for you. Just think of the statistics a moment.

If you are a woman, maybe there are more women than men in your city, but what does that have to do with anything? You only want one man, don't you? Or maybe a few to chose from? The point is, no matter what the statistic, it doesn't have to be affecting you or your situation.

If it seems there are no good men or women currently single, remember there can always be good men or women coming out of marriages, or coming into your view. Just because it didn't work with some other mate, it doesn't mean s/he might not be the perfect mate for you. Again the inner belief, or point of view on this, is crucial.

Recently, I worked with two separate women clients. Both were attractive, in their early forties. One I'll call Sally, was still married, but was about to get out of that marriage. She had raised children, and was active in a folk dance group and other activities. She had some skills to get a job so was not worried in that area. She had been the child of an alcoholic father and had replicated him in her husband.

In coming to me, she simply wanted to make sure the next mate she chose would not bring that problem along again. At the time she came in, she had no fewer than three men she liked, waiting for her to become available. Men were drawn to her liveliness and her acceptance of them. She had lost forty pounds, but still had another twenty to go, so she was not attracting men because of a perfect body.

The other woman I'll call Mary, had been married to a computer company executive. She had divorced him when her son was seven, as she said, "basically out of boredom." They had been divorced for about seven years. He had remarried, and was providing a very nice home for their son.

She saw him as "having it all." He had a beautiful home, their son, and another wife taking her place. As she focused on her lack, he became more powerful in her mind. The more she focused on her lack, the more certain she was that she could find no one in the world to love her. It seemed as though everyone else could have a happy relationship. She could not.

Every man she went out with she perceived as *only a friend*, or *the chemistry just wasn't there*. Worse yet, she may have been attracted to him, and *he never called back*. This is a habit of mindset too. Her own feelings of low self-worth were mirrored by the men.

This kind of programming is not at all limited to women. As Groucho Marx exclaimed, when invited to join an exclusive club,

"What? Me join any group that would have me?" The man I spoke of in Chapter 7 was certainly identical in some of his background to Mary. He believed that there was never the right woman there for him and, of course, there never was. Complete misery!

Remember, loneliness is focusing emotionally on the lack of someone, or group of someones, in your life. You can be physically alone, but you don't have to feel lonely.

My clients with a loneliness problem, also have usually had inner unacknowledged reasons to keep people away from them. You may be used to being in control of your time and your space and may not really want to take responsibility for someone else in your life.

It reminds me of a friend I had when I was about ten or so, Jane, who was lonely for a dog. She was an only child, had never had a pet of her own, and wanted a dog very badly.

My family had a big dog and a cat and my mother always let me rescue and at least temporarily adopt animals. Jane's parents finally agreed to let her have a collie and I went with them when they went to get it.

The dog was beautiful and friendly, and I couldn't believe it when she suddenly told her mother she didn't want it. I never knew what was going on in her mind, but I suspect the reality of the responsibility was too much for her. She would have had complete charge of its care.

Another of my clients, I'll call Joyce, was lonely. She had a good job in the computer industry, and was about 45 years old. She had a daughter in college, and enjoyed ballroom dancing regularly as a hobby.

She told me the ballroom dancing group was full of intrigue and gossip and she never dated anyone there. She also had a semi-relationship for years with a bachelor who took her for granted. They liked the same sport, and sort of *hung out* together. It was working fine for him. It was not working fine for her.

The roots of her staying separate and single were in her family programming. Her parents and other members of her family were literally afraid of outsiders. They were very solitary, and never had people visit without going through great fear. She told me they would turn out the lights when someone came to the door until the person went away. They would do this even when they had invited the person over! She realized this was all strange, and had worked to make her life different.

It was not different enough. She had a lot of rationalizing to excuse why she never liked to have anyone over to her house. Of course, there were good reasons why she should not risk actually going out with someone who would ask her either.

After we released the inner mind prcgramming that was holding her back, Joyce enjoyed quite a social life. Her bachelor friend became very threatened as she became more independent. She even went out with the dance instructor (although he showed he was even more threatened by dating than she was).

She found that she could have all the social life she wanted, when she wanted it. She also found she never had to be lonely again!

Let's get rid of what might be keeping you lonely!

**I release my belief, perception, and judgment that I need to feel lonely because ...**

... I haven't found my right mate yet.
... my mate left/divorced me.
... my former mate has found someone else.
... everyone, or anyone else I know has a mate, or a family.
... I was happy in a former relationship.
... I have never had a happy mate relationship.
... my mother/father was lonely.
... anyone else in my family was lonely.
... I told myself I'm lonely, and I'll always be that way.
... anyone else told me I'd always be alone.
... I'll get attention, or love if I'm lonely.
... I should be punished by being lonely.
... of any conflict in my life.
... I have been lonely in the past.
... I have been traumatized in any way.
... of any past life or pre-life experience.

**I release all need or desire to feel ...**
... lonely for any reason.
... out of control in my social life.

**I release all unwillingness to ...**
... let someone into my life.
... share my life.
... risk having social contacts.

There is another deeper meaning to all kinds of loneliness. It is rooted in the inner belief that you are separate in the world and separate from your maker. This comes especially with our Judeo-Christian mindset and the Garden of Eden story. Through Adam and Eve, we were thrown out of Paradise. Now here we are, compelled to wander the earth... alone.

It also follows from this thinking that we are separate from each other. If we are separate from each other, then we are vulnerable, and always... alone.

As I will discuss more deeply in the next chapter on God, it is this belief in separation that keeps us imprisoned, feeling separate and lonely.

Remember, make your own Releasing Statements that are appropriate to *your* beliefs about your lack and loneliness. It is your beliefs that are keeping your where you are. Get rid of them and open up to the relationships you really want.

## Chapter 11

# Oh God!

Why do we need to drag God into this? What does your idea of God, or lack of God, have to do with your happiness or success? Possibly quite a bit.

Our concept of power in our lives, or lack of power, is linked to whatever idea of ultimate power we can conceive. Does that ultimate power source care about us, and will we get any help from it if we ask? Can we tap into the power? Is there a secret key?

Not only power is at the bottom of our desire for God. There is our innate need to make sense out of our lives. I am not here only by chance. I have a mission. I have a reason to *be.* All the suffering I go through is for something. I am not simply at the effect of winds of chance. I personally have often said, "I can stand on my head for a long time if I know why I'm doing it, or have chosen to do it. I can barely get off the ground though, if I don't know why!"

All religions are based on the assumption that if we follow this or that belief, or teaching, we will be able to become closer to this mysterious source of our being, and the power of life.

If we have all-powerful protection, or all-powerful assistance, we can be safe, or will be able to overcome our problems. We will be able to be free from the problems of humanity, or at least be better able to bear our burdens.

None of us can *prove* the existence of God. I certainly wouldn't attempt it, but I believe there are *useful* and *not-so-useful* beliefs about God and His/Her/Its nature. There are many books that set forth the benefits of this religion or that. My purpose here is to suggest what may be useful to *you*, the reader, whether you think you have any conscious beliefs about God or not.

It is easier to use *The Releasing Strategy* if you have some grounding in spiritual truths. If you have faith that there is something bigger than yourself that can take over in times of stress, you are using a type of Releasing already. In the movie *Star Wars* when Luke let the Force take over to assist him, he was Releasing. Whenever you "let go and let God," you are Releasing.

I must mention an experience I have had to illustrate this thought. I attended a Firewalk experience in 1984. We were living in Atlanta, and this was the first time Tony Robbins, the then not-well-known seminar leader, had come to town. I had read about people walking on hot coals and had decided that I would do it whenever I got the chance. It was such a demonstration of true Releasing it was helpful for me to just work with the concept with several of my clients. When I might be asking them to let go of symptoms, or the need to keep a physical problem, it helped to be able to point out that people were even now defying the laws of the physical world by this very direct act.

When I heard about this seminar that Friday afternoon, I went directly from appointments at my office to the hotel where it was being held. My husband was in California, and neither he nor my children knew where I was. I was alone, so to speak, in the crowd. I definitely planned to walk on the burning coals, but I expected to be hypnotized, or somehow rendered unconscious so I would not have to deal with the very real possibility of injury.

Throughout the evening we went through various visualization and relaxation exercises, and finally Tony said, "Everyone here (there were 160 of us) has given me a sign that they're ready to do the walk." "Oh great," I thought, "I'm at the back of the room. Maybe he didn't see me. Worse yet, maybe I've fooled him into thinking I'm in some state that I'm not."

We rolled up our pants legs, took off our shoes, socks or hose and walked barefoot out to the parking lot where we had earlier helped light two large bonfires of oak wood. They were now bright glowing coals being spread on about 15 ft. long strips of grass sod to avoid melting the asphalt of the parking lot.

Oak wood, as we had learned in the seminar and my firemen clients have confirmed, burns between 1200 and 2000 degrees Fahrenheit. I could vouch for its intensity as I stood near it now and watched Tony's assistants spreading the coals with wheel barrows to make 3 ft. wide and 10 ft. long strips of red hot coals. It looked like a long barbecue pit.

Barefoot like the rest of us, Tony started across first, and then was followed by his assistants. The rest of the crowd lined up at each of the sod strips to take turns. I got in line, and as I nervously arrived at the third position, I decided to drop out to take another look.

Amidst the cheering as each person made it across safely, no one noticed where I was. Each person was handling his own challenge.

I studied the coals again, and the people crossing them on bare feet. I finally got back in line and started working my way toward the coals. Again, I found myself dropping out at about the third position. My mind was in complete conflict and fighting terror. Everything I knew to be true about the physical world was being challenged. Yes, I had thought that certain people, yogis, or other specially trained people could do this, but it seemed incredible to be able to walk barefoot safely on red hot coals after just a few hours of a seminar.

Finally, I decided that I couldn't understand how it was happening, so I would just *do* it. It was almost a toss-up whether I'd go through with it or not. Probably my Scottish nature reminded me I would be wasting my fee for the evening if I didn't.

I got in line again, and this time I got up to the grass, and Tony said, "Okay, you're ready." I looked up as we had been instructed, but just before I took the step onto the coals, I silently said, "Okay God, I absolutely can't do this, you'll have to do it for me! I give up."

I stepped onto the coals, and slowly walked their length. As I looked up at the moon, it was as if I was out for an evening stroll. There was absolutely *no* heat coming from the coals to my feet. Something was protecting me and I felt completely relaxed.

Just before I got to the end, I suddenly thought, "I must remember to wipe my feet on the grass (as we had been instructed), or my feet could be burned." At that moment, the step I was on suddenly became very hot, as if I had just stepped on a hot sidewalk. I immediately pulled my mind back to its former state, and stepped off the coals. I did not even have a blister form.

I had walked barefoot over the 10 feet of glowing coals in a state of transformed consciousness. I now see this amazing experience as another example that we have the power within ourselves to accomplish seeming miracles if we are willing to release control to a greater power within us, whatever name we may call that power.

Anyone who argues that the coals are not hot, or that our feet sweat to keep them from burning, is missing the point.

There will always be arguments as to why we can put aside the laws of physics by Releasing our beliefs about them. It seems that when we fully commit to letting go when we start to walk on the coals, some kind of force field comes into effect around the foot. That is the closest I can come to describing the action.

Think what we could accomplish if we could stay free from the fears that normally run our lives. This is exactly what I hope you're learning to do here.

Think about your image of God. When we work with you as a client, we obtain the percentage of negative feelings from your inner mind about God *as you perceive Him.* We then get the reasons for those beliefs and release them. We have found there are many common reasons for negative feelings about God.

Let's try a few here. Remember that if you have trouble saying the Releasing Statement, that's a good sign we're getting a closely held belief. Just repeat it until it becomes easy to say. You can then release other negative beliefs that come up for you as you try to say a Releasing Statement.

**I release my belief, perception, and judgment that** …

… God is too hard to understand.

… God is too distant from me or my concerns.

**I release my belief, perception, and judgment that…**

**I release my belief, perception, and judgment that…**

… God doesn't care about me.

… God isn't real, or relevant in my life.

… God shouldn't let bad things happen in this world.

… God is a fraud.

… God is responsible for the pain in the world.

… God has left me alone, and helpless.

… I should be able to understand better than I do about what God is up to .

… God wants to punish me, or keep me from happiness.

… God is responsible for any injustice.

… God is not Love.

… I should have any fear about God.

… God doesn't love me just the way I am.

… God has created Hell.

… God isn't supporting me in everything I do or want.

… God has taken anyone, or anything away from me.

… God will ever take anyone, or anything away from me.

… I will die.

There is a great interpretation of the Garden of Eden story that I would like to include here. I don't know where I read or heard it, but it helps to make more sense of Bible teachings: "When we ate of the knowledge of good and evil, we created Fear and started worshipping it."

Isn't that great? It's a definition that makes sense of some other admonitions such as "Have no other gods before Me," and "God is jealous." It also makes sense that we would have to leave our existence of perfect peace and plenty, because we had invented fear to share our world.

Therefore, God didn't throw us out of the Garden, we took ourselves out with our beliefs, perceptions, and our judgments. It is only our judgment, based on our beliefs and perceptions, that keeps us in our paradise, or our hell. With *The Releasing Strategy,* we can recreate our Garden, and be peaceful even in this world, now!

There is another metaphor I would like to include that I feel is so helpful in getting a handle on ourselves and how we view life. This story was brought to me by one of my clients who had been in a workshop given by Ken Wapnick, the head of the Foundation for *A Course in Miracles,* based in New York.

Since it is a second hand repetition, I take no responsibility for its being an accurate quote. Anyway, it goes like this ...

In the beginning, we were all hanging out with God ... just being, when someone said, "Is this all there is?" And at that thought, we created all the lives we've ever had or ever will have and we put them on video tape!

Now what we are really doing is sitting in a darkened movie theater in a chair with a button to push on each arm rest. One button is to select a movie (or a life) to be involved in. As we throw it up on the screen, we become instantly involved in our drama. This is so real!

The other button, when pressed, is for correction by the Holy Spirit, or forgiveness, or Love. We are usually way too involved in our *story* to pay much attention to this other button, but it's always available.

There are some people who have gone from the movies out to the lobby and they are eating popcorn. These are people like

Jesus, Buddha, and other spiritual types. Every so often one of them will open the door and say "Hey there, won't you come out and have some popcorn?" And, of course, we say, "Shshsh... I'm just in the exciting part, someone is hurting me, or I am getting my revenge, or I am being rescued, or I'm rescuing someone else." Endlessly we are involved, so we can't be distracted by popcorn or anything else!

Now, when we *all* get tired of the movies, and go out to the lobby, then we will be able to join hands and *walk out into the sunshine*.

What else is there to say? Now you know what it's really all about!

Chapter 12

# Letting Go of Job Stress

One way to free yourself from job stress is to quit and take a different job, or move to another location within the company. You could call this running away, but it would solve the problem at least temporarily.

There is a wonderful little book by Karen Pryor on behavior modification, published in 1986, called *Don't Shoot the Dog*. The title refers to one method of putting an end to a problem by eliminating the situation or problem completely. Divorce, and quitting a job, are other examples.

If you don't deal with the cause of your stress, however, you will likely find it again when you enter another situation. The boss's traits you hated will emerge with another name and face. You will find him as surely as if you were consciously looking for him or her.

Why do we have so much trouble? You can look again at where you got your original training in your attitude toward authority, and your feelings about whether other people support your work or accomplishments.

Did your parents or other important family members teach you that you were creative and responsible, and intelligent or clever? In school, did teachers reinforce your self-image by impressing upon you that you were very able and creative, and that you could accomplish whatever you wanted to? Did they help you acquire the skills and knowledge that lend real substance to a positive self-image?

Did they at least infer that you could always be depended upon to do the job? Did they praise you for your contributions? What reinforcement did you get for believing that you could trust authority, or that authority trusted you? Did you possibly get the opposite messages through your childhood?

If you are a woman, did you get the message that what is always really important about you is not what kind of job you do, but how you look? Do people around you like you? Are you accepted, popular, pretty? Will you win the football hero, or some other powerful male so you can have the fairy tale life?

If you saw your mother in a supporting role, did you end up in a support job like secretary or nurse because you shouldn't or couldn't think of becoming a businessman or doctor? Now that you are in that lower paying support job, and you have a child or two, you may not have the man in your life to provide for you. You may be under tremendous stress as you try to be a good employee and mother at the same time.

Even if you are a man in the same position of trying to raise a child alone, you will not have the same stress as a woman because she is supposed to be able to be a good mother *no matter what.* She is *supposed* to put her children first .The father who is alone can't be faulted for mistakes with the children. After all, it's not really his job!

If you are a man, your job is usually the central point of your life. It is where your real self-worth is centered. Since you do not have the innate female biological sense of worth (she can bear children), your identity has to come from power in the outer world.

And what, argh, if you haven't found any power in the outer

*or* inner world? You may become bitter and angry and full of blame about why *you didn't make it*.. Alcohol or other drugs may be the only solace for you as you drag yourself through life.

What if you are in sales, and you face rejection every day? Sales is really an unnatural profession. Who likes to be rejected? No one, of course. But if we can clear out the inner mind programming that springs up when we are refused a sale, or when we are encounter resistance, we can continue in the job and be successful.

Remember, to be successful in sales, you don't have to sell everyone. You only have to be able to convince a modest number of people to buy what you are selling and you will be a winner. Most people are not willing to risk the amount of refusals it takes to get to the successes. As Denis Waitley has put it, "Winners make a habit of doing the things that losers don't want to do."

One client and friend of ours in Atlanta was a salesman. Pete had a hidden ceiling on his earnings in sales even though he was a professional of many years. He was persistent and steady, loved his work and would do whatever it took to succeed in commission sales. Still, he could never top $30,000 per year. It was the early '80s and this was not impressive even then.

We found in Pete's case there was an obscure imprint from his parents when he was five years old that was creating the underlying holdback. It seems he had overheard his parents criticizing his aunt for having made $30,000 that year. This would have been in the mid 1940's so the amount would have been impressive. There probably was a bit of jealousy at the base of their discussion. His parents' reaction to the aunt's success made it sound to the young child that she must have been doing something immoral or illegal in order to make so much money.

As an adult, whenever Pete's earnings would approach the magic forbidden total, he would go fishing, change jobs, or get sick. Until he released them, his inner mind employed a variety of ways to avoid earning or producing more than the unconsciously dreaded $30,000. One of the most important reasons was that the self-induced income ceiling, in his mind, *protected him* from losing love and respect.

There is also the issue of aptitudes. You may not be sure what kind of job you should really be in. If so, you're certainly not alone. Most people are in work they took because the jobs were available. Very few have actually looked for work with job satisfaction as a prime consideration. Most look initially to make a living and don't worry about satisfaction until later.

Carefully review your own work history. How – actually – did you come to be doing the work you do? What do you think of this process that got you where you are?

You may want to take the Johnson O'Connor Foundation's battery of tests. These are excellent and will clarify your inborn aptitudes. They have found through over 60 years of testing that if you are in a position that calls for aptitudes that you do not possess, you will be frustrated and unhappy. Likewise, if you have aptitudes you are not using, you will also feel frustrated and unhappy.

If you can't get to one of the Foundation's centers in this country, or if you feel you can't afford to get tested, here is a simple way to test yourself about some of your aptitudes. Answer these questions: What is easy for you? What kind of activities are so enjoyable for you that you'd feel almost guilty if someone were to pay you for engaging in them?

These are the aptitudes that you may overlook because they have always been there. If you develop skills using these talents, you will be happier and more satisfied with your work.

If you do not develop them, you can let them wither on the vine. You will still always have them, but you will be continually frustrated because other people move ahead of you as they develop their talents and practice their skills. Talents are simply the basis you have to build on.

Remember the story in the Bible. The steward who buried his talent for fear of losing it, lost. You must risk something to have what you want. You must risk at least the time and energy it takes to develop learning and skill.

One of my clients had literally spent his life waiting for his life to begin. At 62, he was deservedly depressed. He had not made use of his college education but had worked as a laborer for thirty years because it was secure situation. He had even been afraid to commit to a personal relationship, and so there wasn't even anyone to care whether he lived or died. If you wait until you get things *perfect* before you act, you will wait your life away.

Job stress comes in many different forms. One of my doctor clients, a highly educated specialist, normally worked ten or more hours a day. Jim was 31, and was happily married. He had bought into a good practice and was building it much larger than his partner had ever dreamed. He was respected by his referring doctors and his patients. In general, he had his life going just the way he planned. What was his stress? He was programmed to continue working *just this hard* for 25 more years. He felt like a workhorse that would never get out of the harness.

Jim was easier than many people for me to work with. He was very goal oriented, and when he saw the direction we were going with Releasing, he used his power to focus on removing the blocks. He learned to relax and actually enjoy the life he was creating.

Another client, Tim, came to me when he was feeling frustrated about his work. He had a college education (a degree in marketing) and at 35 was a very successful house painter. He was booked up 12 weeks in advance, from only word-of-mouth referrals. His problem was his father, a bureaucrat who had invested his money in California real estate and was now financially well-off..

This prosperous father constantly told Tim he was just fooling around, and was wasting his life. He simply couldn't understand that Tim was talented and happy in his business. Tim, underneath, had bought into his father's opinion that what he was doing was not worthwhile. He came to me in order to clear up his anger at his father's dictatorial attitude. While he was at it, he also cleaned up his inner belief that his life's work was unacceptable.

A client named Greg worked for a wonderful company and he knew it. He was a mathematician and computer design analyst. The company paid well, and was known for showing its support of employees from company-run insurance to seminars. Everything should have been great. However, there can be personality problems in the best companies, and people with difficult personalities sometimes get promoted to their level of incompetence.

This had happened to Greg's immediate boss, who was a friend of a man promoted into the upper echelons who saw to it that his old friend was promoted too.

This supervisor was not in the job because of his ability to manage people. Being good at pleasing a boss does not guarantee that you have any aptitude for leading or managing people. Sadly, this was the case with Greg's boss. His personality alienated his staff so much that key people were transferring out of the department.

Greg didn't want to leave his job, but he had to endure tantrums by the supervisor who also took a dislike to him. He attacked Greg verbally and tried to make him wrong whenever he could. There is almost nothing so stressful as outright attacks by a superior at work. Greg almost quit.

In clearing up Greg's stress, I found that he had a recurrent program running through all his relationships, including a long marriage (now ended) and other family relationships. He could never let himself get close, and would never get angry with his wife or family. Instead, he would "space out" emotionally, or simply leave if anyone became angry with him.

Greg's father and mother had divorced when he was young and in the extended family where he grew up, his father was always spoken of as "the worthless, no good ...." The family didn't understand that their only son was having to deal with their bad feelings. He grew up and went away, and as he became a father, he avoided fights rather than be the "no good..." that his father was. Now, he was challenged to fight for his survival in his job.

As we released his reactions to this attacking boss, along with the negative beliefs he held about his father, he came to be able to deal with his supervisor in a calm manner. He let the boss's problems be the boss's problems!

So, now are you ready to pull yourself out of the morass of glue that may be holding you in job stress? Let's give it a try.

**I release my belief, perception and judgment ...**
... that I can't stand my job.
... that my job is killing me.

**I release my belief, perception, and judgment that...**
... I won't be able to succeed in my job because of my boss.
... that I have to stay in this job if I have no satisfaction in it.
... that I can't find another job if I leave this one.
... I have to feel stressed if people around me are stressed.
... that I can't have freedom within my job.
... that I can't have satisfaction in my present job.
... I have to hate my job because my parent hated his/hers. ...
... that I can't stand up for myself if I'm attacked unfairly.
... that I have to feel upset if anyone around me is upset.
... I can't remain calm regardless of my surroundings.
... that I have to respond to pressure negatively.
... that I can't enjoy pressure as challenge.
... that I can't create the job situation I want.

**I release all fear ...**
... that I can't be happy in my work.
... I can't find a job where I'm appreciated.
... that my happiness depends on anyone else.
... that I can't be successful in my work.
... that I am guilty if I am successful.
... I'm stuck in my job.
... that there are no opportunities for me.

**I release all need or desire** ...

... to feel upset about my job.

... to feel insecure around ________________ at my job.

... to worry about my job, or my future there.

Now let's take a look at your feelings about success.

## Chapter 13

# Achieving Your Success

Recently I spoke before an organization in San Francisco called Experience Unlimited. This is a non-profit organization to serve people out of work or "in transition." It is supported by the state under the Employment Development Department or EDD, and provides lots of assistance for the people involved. They bring in outside speakers as one of these services. That is how I happened to be there to speak on "Inner Mind Success." There have been speakers on communication, on what a head-hunter wants, and other appropriate themes.

One of my former clients referred me to them, and they asked me to talk about the inner mind. Actually, they didn't have much of a clue what I would really talk about. They were just looking for help.

I had about 150 people at the auditorium in San Francisco to hear me. These people, I found, had been out of work an average of six months, some even a year. I had an interested audience!

I taught them *The Releasing Strategy* that you are learning here to keep their heads clear to find the jobs they wanted. I also spoke before the Peninsula branch of the same organization the next week.

Several people contacted me later to tell me they were using Releasing and it was working for them.

One called to say that he and his friend were using it and moving all sorts of old negative beliefs out of their way. He said, "Do you know how powerful this is?" I had to admit, yes, I did.

I bring this up now because I want to help you if you have anything within blocking you from the success you want. Success is one of those destinations that you may be trying to get to without knowing that you are already there. Let me explain that we are all perfect success mechanisms, or we have perfect success mechanisms. We can't help but create perfectly.

What a disgusting thought you say. Yuk! Nevertheless, we have found that you will create exactly what you need in your life to match your inner mindset. For instance, if you have a problem in childhood with the parent of the opposite sex, you will find the perfect replica of that parent to play out the problem so you can have a chance to heal it.

The problem then becomes that you never learned the first time how to heal it, so you struggle with it over and over again. You can go either from relationship to relationship, or up and down within the same one.

You may have thought that if you changed the characters in the drama, it would come out differently. Of course, if your mate would just change, or if the boss would just change, or if you were just different yourself it would be different.

Well, the last is close to the truth. If you would just let yourself become different enough to release some inner beliefs, you can become different! You can have different reactions.

Success is your definition. Is it a certain amount of money? Is it being able to do a certain kind of work, or find a certain job?

You know in your inner self what success is for you. Right now, take a pen and paper and write down what it would look like for you to really be a success! What would it be called? How would others see you? What does success mean in your life? It may simply be to be able to have the perfect garden. It may mean raising your child or children well.

It may be more connected to outer world perceptions. It may mean to have the *perfect* job for you. It may be earning a certain amount of money. Often, it is freedom from worry about money. It may be a reputation. It may be feeling in control of your time and your life. It may be the ability to travel when, where, and how you would like to. Whatever it is, I want you to know that somehow, you can create it, or a reasonable version of it.

There are many good books on visualization and goal setting. There are many paths to creating success. It is necessary to open the door to your inner mind however, before you can march on through it. You must have the self-image to accept your goal before you can allow yourself to have it.

The book *Superlearning*, by Sheila Ostrander and Lynn Schroeder, published in 1979, tells of Soviet studies of hypnotic learning by the Lozanov School in Bulgaria. This hypnotic technique involves playing Baroque music (60 beats a minute) in the background while information that is to be assimilated is read over the music. Students have learned entire languages in a very short time, and there have been other amazing learning achievements.

The methods have been tried in this country with varying success. Clark and I have come to note what we think is the reason that success is not predictable in this or any other method of visualization, hypnosis, affirmations or goal setting.

There is a note in the book that the Lozanov method was used after the *self-image had been altered*. This is a small note, on a very important point!

Unless your self image is changed to accept the new identity, or information, then it just doesn't get in. In other words, if you are a person who doesn't speak Greek and has never spoken Greek, the Greek language doesn't have much of a chance of getting in. To learn Greek fluently, you must alter your identity to be Greek! You must let go of your belief that you are not also Greek. So, there it is again. You must release your beliefs, perceptions, and judgments on the subject that is holding you back.

To get you started:

**I release my belief, perception, and judgment that ...**

... I can't be successful because I never have been.

... I'm not a perfect success now.

... I can't be successful at what I consciously choose.

**I release all fear ...**

... of not being successful.

... of being successful.

... that I will be overcome by success.

... that friends will leave me if I'm successful.

... that I hurt anyone else if I'm successful.

... that I can't be successful at what I want.

... that no one wants me to be successful.

... that I'm not naturally successful.

**I release my belief, perception, and judgment...**

... that it's too hard for me to be a success.

... that I can't have what I want in life because of my family.

... that I can't be successful because of my looks.

... that I can't be successful because of my body.

... that I'm not educated enough to be successful.

... that I'm not smart enough to be successful.

... that I don't have the right credentials to be successful.

... that I can't let go of whatever has been holding me back.

... that success isn't waiting for me.

... that I'm not destined for the success I want.

... that I can't learn what I need to learn to be a success.

... that I can't be successful because of my family

... that I can't be successful because of my background.

... that anything can stop me from being successful.

**I release all unwillingness to ...**

... be successful.

... do what it takes to be successful.

Always remember, you are naturally successful. You have successfully created what you have and what you are. What are you being successful at? You can choose to be successful at what you *consciously* want and are willing to pay the price to achieve.

Now let's see if we can help you handle your addictions or habits.

Chapter 14

# Releasing Addictions and Compulsive Behavior

The real definition of an addiction is not something you have, but rather something that seems to have you. Ken Keyes in his *Handbook to Higher Consciousness* asserts that anything we strongly desire more than survival needs, or food, clothing or shelter is an addictive demand. That is, of course, very strict thinking.

I would say, simply, if you seem to feel helpless, or at effect of a substance, or situation or person, or if you will go to extreme lengths to have it, to ingest, or use it in some way, it is probably addiction. In other words, you are under its control, or you are out of control in relation to it.

Addiction in recent years has also come to include interpersonal relations, and compulsive behavior. You can be addicted to a situation or relationship that is not healthy. If you use a situation or relationship to deny or bury feelings, you can be acting compulsively.

Roger Callahan, in his book, *How Come I Eat When I'm Not Hungry?,* believes the trigger for all addictive behavior is anxiety. We agree. As I have said earlier, the basis for all negative or limiting emotions is fear. Anxiety is simply the gnawing version of outright fear.

When you feel that anxiety, you can reach for whatever eases your pain, or numbs you. For some, it is alcohol or other drugs. Haven't you heard of *drowning your sorrows*, or drinking to *turn off your mind?* Then, of course, we have the all purpose drug called *food,* available for lifelong comfort. You can *eat* until you're numb.

As a child, you may have been given food to reward you, as an expression of love and nurturing. Now as an adult, when you feel threatened or insecure it is so easy to feel better by reaching for fat foods, sweet foods, foods that feel good in your mouth, or taste good.

Is it any wonder that as we increasingly become a society of harried, mobile, disconnected people with more and more stresses everyday, you may reach for a Dove bar, or a hamburger, or other diverting food to put into your mouth? Then, you get to feel guilty about it as you know very well why you are breaking out in fat.

So the only thing to do as you feel guilty or hate yourself for being so weak as to eat these foods, is to eat some more to ease your anxiety about the whole thing!

Caffeine, that marvelous drug in coffee and other popular drinks, is a national and worldwide favorite. One of the most enlightening stories about caffeine was in the book by J. Phelps and A. Nourse, called *The Hidden Addiction.* In it Dr. Phelps tells of being one of the speakers to address a conference on addictions. The people who were in charge of arrangements for the workshop had put out fruit and rolls, but had not included coffee.

The several speakers (not including Dr. Phelps) would not start the program until coffee was not only started, but made. They held up the conference for a good hour. Very interesting unintended demonstration of addictive behavior! Other drugs can't hold a candle to caffeine as to acceptability as well as addictability in most cultures in the world.

Alcohol is also one of society's great addictive substances and much has been written about the subject. Alcoholics Anonymous and similar programs are effective when they work to heal the spirit of the individual with the addiction through forgiveness of self and others. They advocate a version of Releasing or letting go.

There is much evidence now that there is an addictive gene to give you a real susceptibility to being easily addicted. This is the hidden addiction referred to in the book.

Tobacco is very probably the most harmful addictive drug we have, even more than alcohol. Cigarettes are more portable and have been even more available and easier to use almost anywhere than coffee or other caffeine sources. However, this is changing as more and more of the public are educated and have learned about the hazards of secondary smoke. There are more smoke-free environments, and there is more social pressure not to smoke.

When I was growing up, no one considered saying no to someone smoking around you. A typical gift for any occasion was an ash tray. No one had a thought that it might harm an unborn baby. Of course no one knew anything about second hand smoke either. So, it's a brave new world we're in, and one that will help you get off of these harmful addictions!

In our private practice we have had variable success with addictions. I have learned that a crucial factor that predicts whether someone will be successful giving up a harmful habit is if he/she is truly ready, willing or *wants* to give it up. That's the key.

Almost any program will work for most people if that is so. Almost no program will work if it is not so.

I have worked with people who *thought* they *might* want to quit an addiction; or had a spouse who wanted them to quit, or a parent or doctor who told them they should quit. This is never enough. Just the intellectual knowledge that you *should* quit will be going against inner mind instructions.

So, if you're ready to tackle this, let's go!

**I release my belief, perception, and judgment ...**

... that I can't let go of my negative habit.

... that I am my fat self, my alcoholic self, my cigarettes, my addiction.

... that my meaning in life depends on my addiction.

... that I have to have my next cigarette, fat food, _________, etc., right now.

... that I can't have my next fix *later*.

... that I have to eat fat foods, (have _________ ) because of what anyone has said to me.

... that I have to eat fat foods, (have _________ ) because of identifying with anyone in my family.

... that I have to eat, (have _________ ) because of identifying with anyone else.

... that I have to eat, (have _________ ) to punish myself for being addicted or for anything else.

... to punish myself for anything.

... that I have to eat, (have _________ )to ease any conflicts.

... that I have to eat, (have ___________ ) to feel secure, or satisfied.

... that I have to eat fat foods, (have ________ ) because I've done that for so long.

... that I can't change my habits.

... that I have to eat fat food, (have __________ ) because of any trauma in my life.

**I release all fear** ...

... of not eating fat foods, or not having __________ .

... that I can't let go of my addiction.

... that I can't live without __________ .

Remember to go ahead and make up your own Releasing Statements. Let go of the particular addiction running your life. Engage your Will and you can do it!

## Chapter 15

# Making Affirmations Work

I have said earlier that affirmations don't work very well, or often at all. Now I want to teach you how to make them work marvelously! With *The Releasing Strategy*, you have a tool to use anytime, anywhere to empower the words you choose.

For instance, take Coué's famous affirmation, "*Every day and every way I am getting better and better.*" The usual instructions for using an affirmation are to write it down, over and over - about twenty times is average. Then, repeat the affirmation every day for an extended time, perhaps a month. This is to imprint the statement in the inner mind. It is a hypnotic technique and works better if there is emotion added to it, as in the unintentional imprints I have described earlier.

You may notice that there is a similarity of commercial advertising to affirmations. As I have said, it is a hypnotic technique.

So, to make your affirmation really work for you, you can tie the Releasing Statement to the affirmation as it stands. With Coué's famous affirmation, write down and say, "I **release my belief, perception, and judgment** that every day and every way I'm not getting better and better."

As with affirmations, you should listen to your inner response to your statement. Write that down too. Your inner talk will lead you to what else you need to release. So, cooperate with it, and write it down until you don't hear any more resistance to the statement.

If you use Releasing with your affirmations, you will not have to repeat them interminably. Remember, this strategy comes up from underneath the inner mindset, and while acknowledging the resistance, releases it.

As I have said, you do not have to keep repeating the same Releasing Statement as you do an affirmation. You may approach the subject from different angles, but you don't repeat the same statement. I think this keeps the process a lot more interesting. You don't have to keep on hammering away monotonously with the same thought.

Let me give you another example; I have recently received a prosperity affirmation from the Unity Church in San Jose. This is an affirmation to bring in *unexpected income.* The church is asking everyone joining the program to read the affirmation daily, as will the minister and board. This is using the power of the group united in direction to create an even greater good with the statement. This is very potent just as it is and can have powerful results.

## Affirmation For Prosperity

> I believe that God is the source of all supply, and that "Money is God in Action." I believe that my good is now flowing to me so fully that I have an abundance of money to spare and share, today and always. I believe that true prosperity includes perfect health, perfect wealth, and perfect happiness. This word, which I speak in faith believing, now activates a law of Universal Good, and I accept the results! I bless all

the Good that is with me now. I bless the increase. I bless the others in the Unexpected Income Program of our church, and I know that now we prosper together in every way.

As I said, when repeated until it sinks in, this is already a powerful statement. To make it more so, take each sentence of the affirmation and tie the Releasing introduction to it. For instance.....

**I release my belief, perception, and judgment ...**
... that God is not the source of all supply.
... that money is not God in action.
... that my good is not flowing to me now so that I have an abundance of money to spare and share today and always.
... that true prosperity does not include perfect health, perfect wealth and perfect happiness.
... that I am not activating a law of Universal Good.
... that our church and I are not prospering together in every way.

This is just a sample of what you can do. Let's try some more.

## Affirmation: I am Healthy!

**I release my belief, perception, and judgment ...**
... that I am not healthy.
... that I am not getting healthier all the time.
... that I will be sick because I have been sick.

... that I don't heal easily.

**I release all fear** ...

... of being unhealthy.

... of being healthy.

... of being sick.

**I release all resistance**

... to being healthy.

## Affirmation: I am Happy!

**I release my belief, perception and judgment ...**

...that I am not happy.

...that I can't be happy.

...that I shouldn't be happy.

...that I can't be happy regardless of my circumstances.

...that I don't deserve to be happy.

...that happiness is not my natural state.

**I release all unwillingness ...**

...to be happy.

**I release all resistance ...**

...to being happy.

**I release all fear ...**

...of not being happy.

... of being happy.

...that happiness is not for me.

...that no one wants me to be happy.

...that I wasn't always meant to be happy.

...that it's not good for me as well as other people if I am happy.

...that it's not necessary for me to be happy!

## Affirmation: I am Prosperous!

**I release my belief, perception, and judgment ...**

...that I am not prosperous.

...that I shouldn't be prosperous.

...that I'm not becoming more prosperous all the time.

...that prosperity is not natural for me.

...that there is any reason I can't be prosperous.

**I release all fear ...**

...of *not* being prosperous.

**I release all fear**

**...**of being prosperous.

**...**that prosperity is not coming to me now.

**I release all unwillingness ...** to be prosperous.

## Affirmation: I am Full of Energy!

**I release my belief, perception, and judgment ...**

**...** that I am not full of energy.

... that I am not open to energy.

... that I get tired easily.

... that God isn't giving me all the energy I need.

... that nature isn't working through me to give me energy.
... that my body doesn't have all the energy I need when I need it.

**I release all unwillingness ...**
...to have plenty of energy.

**I release all fear ...**
...of not having energy.

## Affirmation: I am Successful!

**I release my belief, perception and judgment ...**
...that I am not successful.
...that I can't be successful.
...that I shouldn't be successful.
...that success isn't natural for me.
...that I'm not able to do the things needed to become successful.
...that I don't always do what's necessary to be successful.
...that success isn't easy for me.

## Affirmation: I have a Happy Loving Mate Relationship

**I release my belief, perception and judgment ...**
... that I don't have a happy mate relationship.
... I can't have a happy mate relationship.
... that I can't handle a good mate relationship.
... that I don't deserve a happy loving relationship.

... that a happy mate relationship only happens to other people.

**I release all fear ...**
...of having a happy mate relationship.
...of not having a happy mate relationship.

**I release all unwillingness ...**
...to have a happy mate relationship.

Now you have the secret to make your affirmations work. Have fun with it. Work out the most important affirmations for you, such as what you really want your life to look like, and who and what you would like to have in your life experience with you. Think about it for some time, and adjust it as desired.

Then, when you have each element the way it should be, make Releasing Statements out of it. It will be dynamite for you. It may be just the dynamite you need to blow out the blocks that have been holding you back from what you want!

## Chapter 16

# Handling Fears and Phobias

I have said several times that all we really need to do is to get rid of fear. I want to make clear that the fear response is to be respected as a survival response. It is certainly useful to get us out of the way of impending danger - as the tiger, or the truck is bearing down on us - we will move, or RUN!

The point is, if you can run, or take appropriate action, do it. If your fear is is imobilizing you, however, release it so you can function again. Too much of any basic drive can be detrimental.

Thinking about writing this chapter has been a bit of a challenge. Anytime you confront fear you can be put up against your own worst assumptions. You can feel tested.

As I have revealed, we have had a chronic experience in our profession of having a lot of work at once, and then little or no work, partly because of using a process that works so fast. Whenever we would be low on clients for awhile, fear would raise its ugly head to challenge me. I have also had the attitude that if someone found us, they deserved to. It was their business.

Remember the cave, and what I said about the female psychological response? When our practice would be slow. I would conserve. I wouldn't advertise, or spend money, or make any efforts to find new business. It would be as if I suddenly had a pot of cash at my disposal, and I couldn't count on any money *ever* again. I would go immediately into nest-protection mode.

Clark, on the other hand, would react to financial challenge by taking action! So male! (As even my ex-husband used to say,

"Do something, even if it's wrong!")

Clark would immediately advertise, contact new people, write, create all sorts of new efforts, while I often would stand in awe of his being able to function. Actually, he might have been responding in the survival mode, but I think it was a healthier or at least more useful response than mine.

Clark, whether it be from his own longer years of survival, or longer years of cleaning up his inner mind, has never seemed as affected by outer elements, or problems of people around him.

I, again, have felt like Counselor Troi in *Star Trek, The Next Generation,* many times reacting empathically to those around me. I have had to avoid getting caught up in others' fears or depression while I worked to remove them.

To repeat, all you're ever dealing with in your negative thoughts is fear. *It is all you have to contend with*. What else ever gives you any trouble in this world? Think about it, if you feel depressed, or upset, there will be fear lurking beneath it. If you feel angry at someone for an injustice, you have to believe the injustice could or did hurt you or threatens you or someone you care about now.

In Zen and other Eastern religions, you learn to detach yourself from the illusions of this world. By seeing the world as an illusion, you can stay out of fear. So simple to say, "Let's just detach from this reality." But oh, it is so tricky to do!

You can immediately start to worry about how you can make a living, or how you can protect your loved ones from pain or hardship. How can you protect yourself and them from the things you see happening on the nightly news or in the newspaper!

There is an endless supply of potential threats you must

protect yourself from. In addition, there are your feelings of righteousness to protect. Like most of us, you can fight to the end for your belief in being right. We're right, You're wrong! That familiar refrain provides the emotional fuel war runs on.

A dandy observation by J.P.Donleavy, quoted in *Life 101*, is worth recalling:

*When you don't have any money,*
*the problem is food.*
*When you have money,*
*it's sex.*
*When you have both,*
*it's health.*
*If everything is simply jake,*
*then you're frightened*
*of death.*

Says it all doesn't it? Hierarchy of values... or of fears. So when you start to feel that you will not be able to have the income, or love, or health you need to survive and succeed with your mission in the world, or when you start to sink for any reason, use *The Releasing Strategy* to pull yourself out of it.

My daughter provides an intimate example of what we can do with this. She recently started a new job as a nanny while she was a student in college. The job, which I'll admit sounded too good to be true, included a paid-for rental of a beautiful condo in Palo Alto, near Stanford University. She felt that God was definitely on her side, and she was on top of the world.

Then, suddenly, the woman who had hired her called to say that she and her husband were splitting up and she would be moving into the condo herself. Her mother would be taking care of the children. So, in one sweeping phone call, Lynne lost her job, her beautiful new home, and was back to square one.

Lynne reacted valiantly for awhile, saying she would get something new soon, but I noticed that more and more she was staying in her room. Finally, after a few days, she came to me and said "Please work with me, I feel absolutely in the pit and can't seem to make myself even call the man who was offering me another job before."

Of course, when I get to work with a family member, it's as a last resort for them. We all know that we should be able to take care of ourselves emotionally, especially without getting help from a parent. We also like to believe we know ourselves far better than any parent so we shouldn't need them. Consequently, I felt honored that she asked, and also knew that it was hard for her to do so.

It didn't take long for us to find the inner mind reasons she couldn't call anyone about another job. There were six reasons, all very natural and logical (remember the inner mind is at least logical in its own way). We slowly worked our way along releasing them, with a fair amount of argument from her as her mind resisted letting go. Finally though, we completed the job and she went off to other things.

About an hour later, I was sitting here writing and a bright shiny creature I hadn't seen since the job loss came into the room, gave me a big hug and said "You're wonderful, I feel so much better."

Nothing had happened outwardly. She still had to contend with the job hunt, but as she put it, "I just feel entirely different. All the depression is gone, and I feel great!"

I want you to have this tool, too.

I have had a variety of clients with symptoms of panic attacks, or phobias of one kind or another. One, I remember, came to me with a fear of putting her head under water swimming. This was bothering her because her husband had just made arrangements to take her scuba diving in the Caribbean. She was taking a scuba class, and had done fine until the instructor had directed the students to get into the water. She had frozen, and could not force herself to put her head under water.

We tracked through her inner mind reasons that were causing the fear. They were all connected to her problems with her mother.

As a teenager, she had seen her mother as oppressive. She herself was very rebellious. She told me of throwing and breaking things to punish her mother for making her stay in her room, or for grounding her as discipline. Nevertheless, she believed she had been impervious to her mother's negative, critical statements and beliefs about her.

We discovered the central imprint that was driving her fear was her mother's repeated saying that her daughter "always made the wrong decisions, and was going the wrong direction!"

She then told me she could never follow directions. If someone told her to turn right, she would turn left. Invariably, she would get lost. She also had a very hard time making decisions.

The fear came very logically from the belief that she could not follow directions under water (a good way to drown), and if she couldn't follow directions, then she would make the wrong decision and do the wrong thing, (also a way to get killed underwater).

We used *The Releasing Strategy* to free her from this teenage fear and she went on her way. She did go scuba diving and had a wonderful time in the Caribbean.

She told me that the scuba instructor was amazed to see her come back and complete the class. He said that in his many years of experience, he had come to recognize when someone had such a block they would not be able to go underwater. He had seen *that look* on her face as he had tried to help her and never expected her to return.

When I recently appeared before Experience Unlimited in San Francisco, I got a chance to help with a lot of fear because, as I mentioned, the average time out of work for the audience was six months.

Remember too, these people couldn't really know what I was going to talk about. The prior promotion referred blandly to just something about making your mind work for success. As the people filled the auditorium, I wondered if I could teach our Releasing in the brief time I had. Would these people *get it*, and if so, what could they accomplish with Releasing?

At the end of the talk we had questions from the group. One question I always hear is, "How do you know that it really works?"

We have a simple but shockingly effective way to demonstrate the power of Releasing. When the inevitable skeptic asked the question, therefore, I requested a volunteer from the audience. The woman who responded was about my size but stronger than I. She said she was a weight lifter and was in very good shape. I had her hold her stronger arm up straight forward from her body. I then asked her to resist forcefully when I pushed down on her arm with my weaker one. As she pushed up, I pushed down with one hand on the arm. It was a good stand off. Then, to show the linkage between her sense of identity and her ability to resist, I had her say her name aloud and tested again. The arm was still strong.

The groundwork was now laid to demonstrate the power of Releasing to change even your sense of identity. I said, "Now say, 'My name is Jonathan.'" She said the phrase, and then I tested the arm again. It immediately went weak. This is especially easy to demonstrate using a name of the opposite sex.

Next, I said, "Repeat after me, 'I release my belief, perception, and judgment that my name is not also Jonathan.'"

This time when I had her say her name was Jonathan, and tested her strength, her arm stayed strong! This is an impressive physical demonstration to show the power of Releasing.

When people in the audience asked if maybe she wasn't trying as hard that time, she told them she was. I suggested they try it on each other. I will urge you to do the same. Try it on a friend. Have someone else try this name test with your arm. You will find the strength goes right out of the arm when you are saying something that you don't believe. You will also find the arm will become strong as you release that belief.

After the talk, I had many people come up to talk with me afterward about the process, and what they could do with it. One woman, in the midst of the group, pushed her way through, said "Thank you," and pressed a little cloth stuffed heart pin in my hand, and then disappeared. I know she *got it*.

The chair of the Program Department later told me they had many favorable comments, but called to tell me about one special one. They have a critique form that the people fill out about the speaker, and one woman had written in her comments, "Now I have something to get me through the day!"

And now you have a tool to help you get through the day, no matter how rough it may be!

**I release my belief, perception, and judgment that ...**

... I have to be afraid because other people around me are afraid or have been afraid.

... fear helps me in any way.

... I should be punished for something by being afraid.

... anyone wants or needs me to be afraid.

... I can't see that people I'm afraid of are afraid too.

... I have to be afraid because of any experience I've had.

... I have to be afraid because of anything anyone has said to me, or that I have told myself.

... I can't handle anything life comes up with to challenge me.

**I release all need or desire ...**

... to be afraid.

... to feel fear helps me.

**I release all unwillingness ...**

...to let go of my fear about ________________ .

...to feel secure about ________________ .

...to feel safe about ________________ .

Now, let's see how you can use *The Releasing Strategy* to create your life with purpose.

## Chapter 17

# It's a Wonderful Life

Life is wonderful if you feel you're creating it the way you want. What is the meaning of life for you? Do you feel that you have a mission? Do you feel you are accomplishing it? Or, do you feel you are just filling an extra seat at life's table, that there is no real place for you, and you're not needed or desired? Was it probably an accident you happened at all?

In our one-on-one work with a client's inner mind we ask the question, "In percentage, how strong is your fear of not accomplishing your life mission?" Many people are surprised to find they have any response to that question. They often have no conscious clue what they are doing with the life they are living, and no idea if they have a mission at all.

I can't emphasize this too much. If you don't feel you have some purpose to be alive, you won't have the courage to keep dealing with life. It can overwhelm you.

As Scott Peck says in his book, *The Road Less Traveled*, "Life is difficult." But, once that is accepted, then, it is less so because you won't keep telling yourself that life shouldn't be the way it is. You won't feel that life has singled you out for pain.

As soon as you think someone you see or know has it so easy, or you think you want their life to be yours, you can be sure they have problems you would not choose.

Recently, I had another occasion to see this. I have a neighbor who I always thought enjoyed the perfect life. He is the same age as I, has a good job (technical sales), and his wife was also successful as a mortgage loan officer. They had a lovely home, entertained, and had a good relationship with their grown children. You know, a nine-to-five successful, *nice* existence, the all-American life.

With the ups and downs of our kind of business, I would look at Dan and think, "Yes, I am dedicated to my life's work, but, maybe, I should have been smarter and chosen something more like this. What am I doing wrong?"

Then, one day this spring, Dan saw me outside (we often meet at our driveways) and said that his wife had cancer and it had come out of remission. He said she had been dealing with it for 26 years, so it had seemed to me, in my ignorance, that they must have the disease under control. I had not seen her very often, so as the next several weeks went by, and I would ask how she was doing, I didn't worry when he would say, "Well, she's holding her own", and "We're taking it one day at a time."

Then, one evening as my husband and I were walking our dog at the park down the street, we saw Dan there too, as we often do. We were talking about nothing when he said, "Oh, I should tell you, Peg passed away last Friday."

My mind came to a screeching halt. I couldn't have heard what I heard, but, I did! His wife had handled her death with immense courage, living at home and dealing with the pain with help from her doctors and Hospice. She did it the way she wanted to, without any fuss from anyone. She didn't even let him notify the people she worked with until after the funeral.

All this was going on while Dan continued with his work, and was always the cheerful neighbor.

So, the point, of course, is – don't think you know anything about someone else's life or circumstances, and don't offer to trade lives with anyone, even in your mind, because you might get something you didn't bargain for.

Your challenges are yours for most likely good reasons. The negative judgments, you can release. You have a much better chance of handling your problems if you keep clear of the belief that they should be different.

To illustrate: Who has the better chance of emerging alive from a plane wreck in the desert, a person who cries, "It shouldn't have happened! It shouldn't have happened!" or someone who calmly asks, "Okay, where are we now and what's the best way to get out of here?"

Research by Israeli psychologists Mario Mikulincer and Ilana Peer-Goldin (*Brain Mind and Common Senee,* August, 1992) indicates that "Happiness, at least in the short term, occurs when we approximate our ideal visions of ourselves ... When we see a wide gulf between our reality and our ideal, we are probably most vulnerable to general depression, sadness and dissatisfaction (the flip side of happiness)."

"... Falling short of others' expectations, on the other hand, is more likely to produce feelings of guilt or anxiety (as opposed to peace of mind.) Assuming the role of the ideal self led to happiness; corresponding to one's *ought* self (the nagging portrait of how we think others expect us to be) led to something close to tranquillity and security."

If you are living your ideal life, or close to it, you will be able to withstand the anxiety or guilt that may come from not living the existence that others may expect of you. This is how the solitary writer or inventor can function for years without society's or even his family's approval. He is happy because he is living according to his own light, his inner ideal self.

In our one-on-one work I have had many people find this issue one of highest importance. Again, many are caught up in the belief that what they are currently doing can't possibly be part of the mission they should be accomplishing. It's like being an actor and feeling you are alive only when you are in a production. There are many people waiting and waiting for their life's mission to show up, while their lives drift away!

There is an old saying, "Bloom where you're planted." If you want to find your life mission you can look at the happiness and satisfaction you feel in your day-to-day existence. If you often feel happiness, then you are living your life's ideal. If you feel satisfaction, you are at least living the way you perceive others may need you to live.

For instance, even if you are a computer programmer, you may feel your life's ideal is to be climbing great mountains. If you don't do it, or at least train and plan for it, you will always feel lacking and depressed.

It would be best if you got involved in some way with your ideal activity and discover if it still calls. Instead of dropping everything at once, try out smaller commitments. Do something close to home, and broaden out from there.

You could take mountain climbing lessons on your vacations. You could build your body at local gyms. Then, after you prepared, and organized your efforts, you could get involved climbing those mountains.

As a spiritual seeker, you may feel that you have to go to Mecca, or to an ashram in India, to accomplish your life mission.

But you may have a child counting on you to provide a livelihood. Should you drop the child off at an orphanage to go following your dream? Maybe. Some people have done just that.

On the other hand, it's hard to find real happiness on the back of another's pain or loss. This is where tranquillity and feelings of security come into play. If you perform the duties required of you, often in a strange way, you will find your dream opportunity will come to you at a later date when everything will be perfect.

But what if you don't have any real responsibilities in life, or you have finished a job you had agreed to, and you are free to follow your dream? The question then becomes, *"How do I figure out what my dream is?"*

One way to find out begins with a process described in Chapter 12. If you have aptitudes that you are not using, you will be unhappy. Look to see what activities or situations make you feel happy. This is not to say that a rich or beautiful environment will do the trick. It is not the *things* provided but the opportunity to use your aptitudes or fulfill your inner ideal that will bring happiness.

If you are happy helping people, you may simply give good advice to friends. If you are happy speaking or teaching, you may be fulfilled getting involved with a charitable cause. You will always find places that need your abilities and vision of yourself.

Recently, I got involved with the presidential election and worked to elect my candidate. I had never become so involved politically, and took my time away from important personal things to do it. I worked hard getting voters registered, and then took some time off to concentrate on my own business. Still caught up in it the day before the election, I went down to the Democratic headquarters and said, *"Use me."* They did, and even on election day, I worked to help get out the vote.

I did all this because it was important to me to elect my presidential candidate. Also, I cared about who became the next senators from California, and other issues. (Clark had originally set me on fire with the observation that he took comfort in the fact that as a democracy, we as a people would unavoidably get the leadership we deserved.)

I am mentioning this here because I felt truly *happy* when I finally went to bed on election night. This was not just because *my guy* won, but because I felt his and the senators' winning was truly best at this time for our country.

Nothing was changed in my personal life. Nothing would have been changed if either of the other candidates had been elected. My hope for possibilities, however, for people in this country was opened up again, and the entire business of increasing possibilities for people is part of my life's ideal. (A note if you are a Republican, just ignore politics and use this tool anyway).

Now let's use *The Releasing Strategy* to help you find your life's ideal, or purpose, and accomplish it.

**I release all need or desire ...**

...to avoid my life's purpose.

...to feel that I can't accomplish it.

...to feel I'm not good enough to have a purpose in life.

...to ignore my life purpose.

**I release my belief, perception and judgment that...**

...I cant have a wonderful life!

...my life isn't getting better all the time.

**I release all fear ...**

... of not accomplishing my life purpose.

... of accomplishing my life purpose.

... that I don't have a life purpose

... that I can't see the vision of what my ideal self is.

... of not knowing enough to accomplish my life's purpose.

... of not being old enough to accomplish my life's purpose.

... that I'm not young enough to accomplish my life's purpose.

**I release all unwillingness ...**

... to find my life's purpose.

... to do what I need to do to accomplish my life's purpose.

... to be at ease with myself and my life's purpose.

... to be happy with my vision for myself.

... to feel safe and secure in my vision for myself.

You have learned a variety of Releasing Statements through the chapters in this book. My fondest desire is that you continue to use them and find the happiness within yourself that is there when you remove the excess negative baggage.

I want you to keep that happiness and sense of power in your everyday experiences. You can do it using *The Releasing Strategy* as you go through your day. Now you have the tool. Use it. God bless you, and have a wonderful life!

# Index

To order ***The Releasing Strategy™***, please send $11.95 plus $3.00 shipping and handling (CA residents please add 8.25% sales tax) to:

Watershed Books
2059 Camden Ave. Suite 249
San Jose, CA 95124
(408) 978-3006

____ copies at $11.95 each ($14.95 for Canadians)________
For 2 or more books, subtract 10% discount ________
California residents add 8.25% ________
Basic shipping 3.00 for first book ________
--add $1.00 for each additional book ________
US/Canada first class shipping, add $1.50 to order ________

Name ______________________________________________

Street ______________________________________________

City,__________________State _____ Zip_____________

Check or MO enclosed #__________or

Mastercard or Visa

#_________________________________________________

Exp date _______

Signature_________________________________________

Please allow 3 weeks for delivery.